ISSUES OF CHRISTIANITY

Joe Walker

Hodder Gibson

A MEMBER OF THE HODDER HEADLINE GROUP

Acknowledgements

The author would like to thank Lorna and David whose patience with the writing process was well and truly pushed to the limit this time – especially given that their swimming development hasn't exactly been helped by the number of takeaways this book has spawned.

Thanks also to those who have looked at the book in draft form and made helpful comments along the way. Particular thanks to Dr Michael Purcell, Senior Lecturer in Systematic Theology at the University of Edinburgh who offered valuable insight into both Roman Catholic and Orthodox Christian traditions. Thanks also to Emeritus Professor Joseph Houston, formerly of the Department of Theology and Religious Studies at the University of Glasgow, who was one of my colleagues setting and marking Advanced Higher Religious Studies for many years, and who also has the dubious distinction of being one of the three signatures on the scroll of my first degree in Theology. That Joe helped this Joe keep on track as far as the Reformed Christian perspective was concerned. He was assisted in this by the Rev Paul Beautyman, Church of Scotland Minister and Chaplain in the place where I have my day job, Liberton High School in Edinburgh. Thanks also to Nick Blair, Chaplain and RE teacher at Merchiston Castle School in Edinburgh who represents a more Evangelical perspective, Chris Foxon, Senior Lecturer in RE at Strathclyde University and Methodist Minister, and Frank Quinn, Setter for the SQA at Intermediate 1 and 2 levels as well as Head of RMPS at St Margaret's RC Academy in Livingston. Any mistakes and omissions are entirely my responsibility however, but if you buy enough of the books I'll be happy to put them right in the 2nd edition.

Finally, thanks to Iain Stirling, Chelsey Evans, Chrissie Stevenson, Emma Gunda, Paula Manners, Rachel Manners, Julie Wilson, Emma Collier, Tom Redford, Danielle Atai, Karen Hay, Yee Ling Fong and Susan Traill who, as students at Liberton High School, keep my feet on the ground – daily – while reminding me that in the young people of today there is hope for tomorrow.

Joe Walker

The Publishers would like to thank the following for permission to reproduce copyright material:
Photo credits Cover photo by Oliver Burston/Debut Art; Alamy, pages 114, 131; Andrew Holbrooke/Corbis, page 8 middle; Art Directors, pages 106, 117; Bettmann/Corbis, page 42; Brooklyn Museum of Art/Corbis, page 75; Christian Poveda/Corbis, page 122 top; Claudia Kunin/Corbis, page 8 left; Corbis, page 123; Corbis Sygma, page 7 middle; E & E Picture Library, page 111; Getty Images, pages 61, 81, 117; Hulton-Deutsch Collection/Corbis, pages 60, 71, 122 bottom; Jim McDonald/Corbis, page 67 bottom; John Walmsley, page 67 right; Panos, page 120; Patrick Robert/Sygma/Corbis, page 8 right; Peter Macdiarmid/Reuters/Corbis, page 97; Photodisk, pages 7 left, 13, 17, 67 left and top, 79; Rex Features, pages 7 right, 48; World Religions, pages 100, 102, 108.
Acknowledgements All sources have been acknowledged in the text. All website addresses are correct at the time of publication and have been checked for content. Should you find that a website address changes, or the content is unsuitable, please contact the Publisher, who will be happy to make any changes as necessary.

Every effort has been made to trace all copyright holders, but if any have been inadvertently overlooked the Publishers will be pleased to make the necessary arrangements at the first opportunity.

Although every effort has been made to ensure that website addresses are correct at time of going to press, Hodder Gibson cannot be held responsible for the content of any website mentioned in this book. It is sometimes possible to find a relocated web page by typing in the address of the home page for a website in the URL window of your browser.

Hodder Headline's policy is to use papers that are natural, renewable and recyclable products and made from wood grown in sustainable forests. The logging and manufacturing processes are expected to conform to the environmental regulations of the country of origin.

Orders: please contact Bookpoint Ltd, 130 Milton Park, Abingdon, Oxon OX14 4SB. Telephone: (44) 01235 827720. Fax: (44) 01235 400454. Lines are open 9.00 – 6.00, Monday to Saturday, with a 24-hour message answering service. Visit our website at www.hoddereducation.co.uk. Hodder Gibson can be contacted direct on: Tel: 0141 848 1609; Fax: 0141 889 6315; email: hoddergibson@hodder.co.uk

© Joe Walker 2005
First published in 2005 by
Hodder Gibson, an imprint of Hodder Education, a member of the Hodder Headline Group,
2a Christie Street,
Paisley PA1 1NB

Impression number   10 9 8 7 6 5 4 3 2 1
Year   2010 2009 2008 2007 2006 2005

Typeset in Garamond 12.5pt by Fakenham Photosetting Ltd, Fakenham, Norfolk
Printed and bound in Great Britain by Arrowsmith, Bristol.

A catalogue record for this title is available from the British Library

ISBN-10: 0 340 886706
ISBN-13: 978 0 340 886700

Contents

Contents

Introduction

Christianity in RMPS

In Primary school and early secondary school you should have learned about Christianity – its history, basic beliefs and practices. You may have studied Christian festivals and some Bible stories too. Now that you're doing Intermediate 1, 2 or Higher we want you to go one step beyond what you've done so far. This book is designed to get you thinking about the ideas behind Christianity – its theology, its philosophy and the beliefs which lie underneath it all.

More than that this book aims to get you thinking. Christianity, like all world religions offers you a challenge. This book aims to challenge you with the things Christians do and believe. It will hopefully provoke you into thinking more clearly about your own views. It is not just designed to help you pass your exam – though that would be nice – it is designed to get you thinking about the big questions of life and the big issues by presenting Christian ideas on these topics.

The book has different ways of trying to get you thinking:

Text: There is explanatory text about the issues. Hopefully this is deep enough to cover things adequately, but light enough not to give you cranial indigestion.

Talk Points: Yes, you're meant to talk about it. Do you really know what the person sitting next to you in class believes? Maybe you will by the end of this course. Maybe while you're talking you'll think of something differently for the first time.

Time Outs: This gets you to really reflect on your thinking about the topics you're studying – or to do something to find out more about it all.

There's no way any one book could teach you everything about one religious faith. It's assumed that you have studied Christianity in your RME class before you do this course. Besides there is no such thing as the one Christian view, but many different views. There's a mass of material out there. Hopefully this book can be your helpful starting point.

Thanks for taking the time to use this book.

Joe Walker

History; Spread; Variety; Healthcheck

What is a World Religion?

A whole book could be written on what is a religion. Do you need a God? – Buddhists don't have one. Do you need to pray? – all religions have different ways of doing this. How should you live your life? – there's as many answers to this as there are religions.

To put it simply, a World Religion is a faith which is represented all over the world – more or less. How can you tell if someone is a member of a religion? It's easy if the person regularly attends a place of worship – but what about those who don't? Many people will often claim to be a follower of one religion or another but then do little about it – or so it would seem.

Statistics regularly show that most people in the UK who are religious are Christians – but what does that mean? Sometimes it's just that they were baptised, sometimes it's because their parents were Christians, and other times it's because they know they're not anything else! How many times have you heard people in school say things like 'I'm a Protestant Sir, does that mean I'm a Christian too?' Following a religion can be something which is central to your life, something you just do out of habit or something you do at certain times – for example, how many people in the UK get married or have funerals in churches but wouldn't really think of themselves as Christians? Even people who are Christians come in various varieties – some study their faith carefully and put it into action – some possibly just go through the motions. It would be interesting to ask many 'ordinary Christians' some of the questions which you will tackle in this book – would they have answers? Would they have thought it through? Does it matter?

When something is a religion, what identifies it as such? It's probably true that the following are common features of any religion – although even that's hard to justify in all cases. A religion most often has:

◆ A set of beliefs involving a central core which all followers have some agreement with: In Christianity this would be that Jesus was the Son of God.

◆ A set of practices which, although they may vary in different cultures and contexts, really boil down to the same thing: In Christianity this would be some kind of welcoming ceremony for entry to the Church.

◆ A set of moral values which, although there will be a multitude of varieties of putting them into practice will come down to the same thing: In Christianity this would be something like the idea that it is a duty for the strong to help the weak.

◆ A shared history or set of traditions: All Christian denominations can be traced back to the first Disciples and all denominations have developed their own versions of practices which these disciples probably originated.

As religions have developed and grown they have often taken in elements of other faiths or cultures and made them their own. This is probably quite a natural development. In Christianity, for example, symbols of Easter are very similar to pre-Christian pagan symbols, and many saints have their origins as pre-Christian 'gods'.

Religions vary in strength and influence throughout the ages. Some claim that the UK can't be thought of as a Christian country any more and therefore the place of Christianity in RMPS should be less central than it once was. This is something which is up for discussion and about which you will maybe develop your own informed view – like everything else you're about to study. Religion has played, and still plays, a major part in shaping the kind of world we live in – so shouldn't you find out something about it?

Talking Point (A)

Is Britain still a Christian country? Was it in the past? Does Christianity have any influence left in the UK? The World?

A Brief History of Christianity

Phew! Where to begin? There are many books about Christian history. There are many different Christian groups today which have developed over the years. The changes came about because of disagreements over beliefs or practices – no different to the disagreements in any family. This flowchart gives you just the bare bones with some of the reasons for changes.

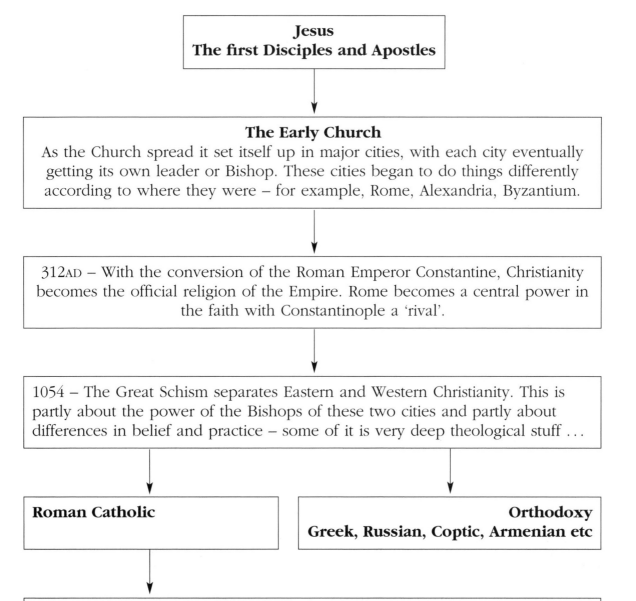

Jesus
The first Disciples and Apostles

The Early Church
As the Church spread it set itself up in major cities, with each city eventually getting its own leader or Bishop. These cities began to do things differently according to where they were – for example, Rome, Alexandria, Byzantium.

312AD – With the conversion of the Roman Emperor Constantine, Christianity becomes the official religion of the Empire. Rome becomes a central power in the faith with Constantinople a 'rival'.

1054 – The Great Schism separates Eastern and Western Christianity. This is partly about the power of the Bishops of these two cities and partly about differences in belief and practice – some of it is very deep theological stuff …

Roman Catholic

Orthodoxy
Greek, Russian, Coptic, Armenian etc

In the 16th Century, Martin Luther begins the Reformation. He protests against beliefs and practices in the Roman Catholic Church (hence the word Protestant). He disagrees with the role of priests and Church Hierarchy as well as doctrines like salvation by works not grace etc. The Roman Catholic Church responds with a counter reformation but by now it is too late and the split between Protestants and Catholics is complete.

Protestants

Church of England

Church of Scotland

Methodist, Quaker, Congregational, Baptist

Free Church

Salvation Army

There are disagreements about how many Christian denominations there are in the world today, but the number is staggering. A look at the following web page will give you some idea. See ***www.nationmaster.com/encyclopedia/List-of-Christian-denominations***. Alternatively type 'How many Christian Denominations are there?' into a search engine and be prepared to do a lot of page scrolling!

Talking Point **B**

Is the fact that there are so many different kinds of Christians a sign of a healthy faith or an unhealthy one?

Christianity in the 21st Century: World – UK – Scotland – Your School

So let's take a snapshot of Christianity today – but remember that who you ask may well give a different account of the statistics below.

About 33% of the world's people are Christians, i.e. 2,015,743,000 of the Earth's 6,091,351,000 population are followers of some form of Christianity.

Top 10 Largest National Christian Populations			
Rank	**Nation**	**Number**	**Percent**
1	USA	224,457,000	85%
2	Brazil	139,000,000	93%
3	Mexico	86,120,000	99%
4	Russia	80,000,000	60%
5	China	70,000,000	5.7%
6	Germany	67,000,000	83%
7	Philippines	63,470,000	93%
8	United Kingdom	51,060,000	88%
9	Italy	47,690,000	90%
10	France	44,150,000	98%
11	Nigeria	38,180,000	45%

Source: www.adherents.com/largecom/com_christian.html

There are 37.3 million people in England and Wales who state their religion as Christian. The percentage of Christians is similar between the two countries but the proportion of people who follow other religions is 6.0% in England compared with 1.5% in Wales.

(Source: www.statistics.gov.uk/census2001/profiles/commentaries/ethnicity.asp)

Religion	England & Wales		Scotland		
	Census	LFS	(current)	(upbringing)	LFS
Christian	77.7	79.9	68.9	79.2	81.9
Buddhist	0.3	0.3	0.1	0.1	0.2
Hindu	1.2	0.1	0.1	0.1	0.2
Jewish	0.5	0.5	0.1	0.2	0.2
Muslim	3.2	3.0	0.9	0.9	0.8
Sikh	0.7	0.6	0.1	0.1	0.0
Any other religion	0.3	0.8	0.6	0.2	0.6
No religion	16.1	13.8	29.1	19.1	16.1
All population excluding 'not stated'	48,031,258	148,540	4,783,950	4,639,149	15,223

In Scotland, the pattern is fairly similar, though this identifies religious people by age as well as in Christianity by denomination.

Religious affiliation by age band
Column percentages, 2001 data

All household members	Under 16	16–24	25–34	35–44	45–54	55–64	65+	All
None	36	36	39	30	26	17	13	28
Church of Scotland	39	38	36	43	49	58	64	47
Roman Catholic	17	16	17	17	14	15	12	16
Other Christian	6	7	6	7	9	8	9	7
Base	7,394	3,578	4,446	5,401	4,996	4,024	6,015	35,854

Source: www.scotland.gov.uk/library5/society/spv5-50.asp

Some 11.2% of the population of Scotland attended church on an average Sunday in 2002.

Four of the smaller denominations have grown in the past eight years: Baptists (24,800 – up 1%), Christian Brethren (18,200 – up 6%), Pentecostals (10,100, up 11%) and the Salvation Army (7,000 – up 8%).

The percentage of church-goers who are men has increased (37% of church-goers in 1984, 40% in 2002) and there has been an actual growth of 1,000 attendees aged 65 or over.

Church-going remained markedly higher in the Western Isles and Skye & Lochalsh where it was still nearly 40% of the population. Ten other council areas had more than the average 11.2% attending on Sunday, of which the highest was Inverclyde with 17%. The Church of Scotland declined 22% between 1994 and 2002, down to just under 230,000 Sunday attendees. Roman Catholic attendance declined 19% in the same period, to just over 200,000. Between them these denominations account for three-quarters of all Scottish church-goers, Church of Scotland 40% and Catholic 35%.

Source: www.scottishchristian.com/features/0305census01.shtml

Talking Point   C

Carry out a census of your school – making sure that responses are anonymous. How many people consider themself to be religious? How many Christians and of what denomination? You could widen this survey out as much as you like – perhaps by asking schools in your authority to do the same. How representative is your school of your age group? How representative is your age group of people in the world in general? Is Christianity strong or weak where you live? Can you really judge it?

Of course there are many more indicators of the state of Christianity that you could use to plot just where Christianity is on the world stage right now. Anyway, some say that facts and figures like these can be used to back up any argument you care to present about the faith. They might argue that even those in Scotland who wouldn't think of themselves as Christians owe a lot to Christian ideas about morality and many other issues. The influence of Christianity in the world is often difficult to pin down. Most would agree, however, that Christianity worldwide isn't dying out by any means.

When we are born our parents have great hopes for us. Some of us turn out to be kind, helpful, generous people who make the world a better place. Others turn out to be nasty, selfish and even brutal. How does this happen? How does an innocent baby turn out to be a mass murderer or a terrorist or a saint?

There are many different views on human nature in psychology or philosophy, as well as in the religions of the world. Humans like to know what makes us tick. Why do we do what we do? Why do we sometimes do things even though we know we shouldn't? How do we tell right from wrong? What should we believe about life? Where do our beliefs come from? Why do we even think up questions like this?

One of the reasons you are doing RMPS is because you are interested in these kinds of questions: What are people all about?; What are we aiming for in life?; How do we get what we can out of our short time here on earth (and is there more 'life' to come afterwards)? This course covers all three of these big questions. You'll know them as:

◆ The Human Condition

◆ The Goals

◆ The Means

Now why would you want to find out what Christianity teaches about these three issues? Surely you should be asking psychologists and scientists and doctors and philosophers? Well, by all means ask them as well.

Christianity, like all religions of the world, has a long history of thinking through these kinds of questions and suggesting answers. It can't force you to accept these answers, but it can get you thinking about your own response to them.

That's what this book is about. There's not much point in just learning a series of facts about Christian belief – it has to make you think about your own views. Christians suggest answers to all these three issues. You can take them or leave them – that's up to you – but you can't if you don't know what the suggested answers are in the first place.

When you look around the world today – watch TV, read the papers – you might be forgiven for thinking that the world's pretty messed up – and that most of that is caused by the actions of humans.

The good, the bad, and the ugly.

When you think back to the last time you did something wrong, you have to ask yourself: Why did I do that? Especially as you probably knew it was wrong even as you were doing it.

What is being a human actually about? Is there such a thing as the human condition? Have Christians got the explanation for this correct? Is what you'll find in this book the key to one of the most important things there is – understanding yourself?

Why does one baby turn out to be a hero and the other a killer? What's the difference between humans and everything else? What is the unique job of humans? What, in fact, is the meaning of life? The Christian faith suggests answers to these questions. Read on.

Getting into it

Think through the following questions – it's up to you and your teacher whether you write answers to them, discuss them, turn them into role play, dramas, essays, pieces of artwork etc.

◆ What is special about being human?

◆ Is there such a thing as human nature?

◆ Are humans born bad?

◆ What's the difference between humans and other life on earth?

- Do humans have special responsibilities?

- Why do humans do good or bad things?

- How do our beliefs affect our actions?

- Are we alone in the Universe?

- Were humans made for a purpose?

- Should we spend any time thinking about human nature or is it a waste of time?

- What is the point of my (yes, your) life?

God and The Creation

> **Recipe for Humans from the *Almighty Cook Book – Divine Dishes***
>
> Take a good planet-full of stardust
> Mix with cataclysmic energy
> Shape the resulting dough into head, body, two arms and legs
> Blow up nostrils with the breath of life
> Imbue with a soul (see recipe number 1)
> Stand back and watch the result mess things up

Why did God create life?

Christians believe that God created everything. This was a choice. He could just as easily not have bothered – enjoying his own company for all eternity. Christians believe that he created life out of love, because he wanted to share the big beautiful Universe with other beings. The Universe is made for sharing. Some think that maybe God would have been lonely without us or that he needed us to make him feel good. Christians don't accept either of these views. For them God is the most powerful thing it is possible to be (or even think about) – he needs nothing. This doesn't make him cold and remote, it makes him even more loving because he could just have kept the Universe all to himself. God also didn't make the Universe out of the spare parts which were already lying about –

Talking Point 1

What do you think of the existence of God? Yes? No? Maybe?

he made it out of nothing ('*ex nihilo*'). Every atom that exists everywhere was made by him from nothingness. God not only made matter, he made time and space too. Where and when did God do this then? Best not to think about that in case your head explodes!

Roman Catholic View

God created us to share His immense love, because love is to give, to share what one has. That is why God created us. God created us to know, LOVE, and serve Him in this world so that we can be eternally happy with Him in the next.

Source: http://truecatholic.bizland.com/book/book.htm#cqa53

How did God create life?

Another tricky one. It has been said that if God explained how he created everything you wouldn't understand it anyway. The Christian Bible tells a story about how it was done, but doesn't get too technical. How much do you need to know anyway? You can get along fine with a computer without knowing how its insides work – why do you feel the need to know God's tricks of the trade?

Christians believe that God's infinite, incomprehensible power explains that he was able to make a Universe and all life in it. The details aren't important. Of course, lots of people nowadays don't like this way of looking at it because it sounds a bit like a cop-out. If God really did it he'd prove it to us by telling us how wouldn't he?

Here's two examples which might make you think again about that:

1 Mervin the magician does incredible tricks. No-one is ever sure how he does it, until one day he decides to reveal all in his new

act. Before each trick he explains completely how he does it. Oddly enough, his audiences start to dwindle.

2 Dr Siegelibuur is a nuclear weapons scientist. His work is top secret. How to make a nuclear weapon is highly dangerous knowledge. One day, tired of the rat race, Dr Siegelibuur shaves his head, becomes a hippy and publishes the instructions for making nuclear weapons in the local paper. Unsurprisingly the world's governments are not pleased.

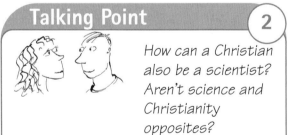

> **Time Out** ①
>
> *Some people think that there's not much point in thinking about how or why the Universe began – others think it helps us to understand who we are and what life's about. What do you think?*

Christians don't think you have to know how God made the Universe, you just have to believe that he did. This is called faith. Faith means that you believe without proof and maybe more importantly you believe even when the facts seem to be going against you. In the past, Christians tried to fill every gap in scientific theories with the explanation 'God did it'. The trouble was, as those gaps in our knowledge got smaller and smaller God got squeezed out. This 'God of the gaps' theory isn't popular with most Christians who have faith that God created everything no matter what science says.

Christians argue that God is above science. Scientific explanations can take us so far but not the whole way. Many Christians are scientists and they're quite happy to accept the findings of science but still believe that in some unknown way it all still comes down to the action of a creator God. Maybe science is thinking God's thoughts after him. One Christian has commented about the whole issue of the creator God:

'It's far less important to love knowledge than it is to acknowledge love'.

God created everything through love. What more do you need to know?

> **Talking Point** ②
>
> *How can a Christian also be a scientist? Aren't science and Christianity opposites?*

Two Slightly Annoying Arguments for Christians

The First Cause Argument

This says that everything needs a cause and that the cause of everything must be God. The argument has its good points, but it has serious flaws too:

◆ It says everything needs a cause except God – why doesn't God need a cause?

◆ It says that things can't go on uncaused forever – why not?

◆ It says that the first cause must have been God – why not some other God (or a group of Gods)?

Time Out ②

Have a class debate on whether 'The Universe needs a cause'.

Christian theologians have gone through hoops throughout the ages to defend this argument. Others have just taken a more basic approach by simply believing that God needs no cause and that only the God they believe in could have been such a first cause. See? Faith again.

Roman Catholic view

Roman Catholics believe that there must have been a first cause because, to put it simply, souls don't evolve:

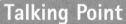

'There was a time when neither man nor any other living thing inhabited this globe of ours; and without pressing the point regarding the origin of life itself from inanimate matter or the evolution of man's body from lower organic types, it may be maintained with absolute confidence that no explanation of the origin of man's soul can be made out on evolutionary lines, and that recourse must be had to the creative power of a spiritual or personal First Cause.'

Source: http://www.newadvent.org/cathen/06608b.htm#IBc

Talking Point ③

Is there such a thing as a soul? Are you your soul? Why do so many of the world's religions believe in a spiritual self or soul?

Got one!

Time Out ③

Carry out a class/school survey into the existence of the soul. Report and discuss your findings.

The Argument from Design

This basically says that if you look around you you'll see evidence of order and beauty in the world and not chaos and disorder. This points to the very good chance that something must have made it that way on purpose. This something must have been almighty. In fact, the Almighty. This argument too has some loose threads:

Beauty and order?

◆ It says everything is designed because it looks that way – why? Just because something looks that way doesn't mean it is.

◆ It says that good design is evidence for the existence of a God – but it ignores evidence for bad design. Does this prove that God didn't design it or was rubbish at designing?

◆ It says that God must have designed everything – why could things not just have developed by chance?

An old Christian saying goes like this:

'When things are good, praise God, when things are bad, trust God.'

Time Out ④

Looking at the world around you, what evidence is there of good and bad design in nature?

Now this might seem like a bit of a contradiction to you, but for Christians it isn't. Christian teaching talks about the *mysterium* of God. This means that how God operates is beyond us and always will be. No point in trying to guess God's next move or work out what he's up to – you just have to believe that he knows what he's doing and let him get on with it. That's what Christian faith is all about.

God's greatest achievement?

At the end of the creation story, God makes humans – man first and then a woman.

GOD MADE MAN FIRST TO SHOW THEY ARE IN CHARGE

NO, THE MAN WAS JUST A TRIAL RUN SO GOD COULD GET IT EXACTLY RIGHT THE SECOND TIME

Talking Point 4

'If God created humans he should have done a better job.' What do you think?

Christians believe that humanity (men and women!) is the high spot of God's achievement in the creation story – the final and most significant act which God carries out. Christians believe that God and humanity share something special which God and everything else in creation doesn't. In humans, God saves the best 'til last.

Having created humans, God then gives them responsibility for naming everything. In Bible times, having the power to name something meant you had power over it. So God must have meant for humans to have power over everything. This power over everything is called 'Dominion' and, depending on how you look at it, is either the greatest blessing or the greatest curse.

Dominion as lording it completely

One understanding of Dominion is that everything in the universe is there for human use. You can do whatever you want with it. This view of the Universe is called anthropocentric because it puts humans right at the centre. If everything is there for us, then what we do with it/to it isn't important. It's ours to do with as we please – a gift from God. This kind of understanding of Dominion isn't going to lead to people joining the Green Party.

Dominion as lording it a little

Some people think everything is for human use, but that doesn't mean that anything goes. You can have power over something but still have a sense of responsibility for it. Your teachers have power over you, but they shouldn't abuse that power. They should use it wisely in a responsible way – for your benefit.

Dominion as a service

Dominion can also mean that what God meant wasn't that you were in charge, but that you are in charge so live up to it well. With great power comes great responsibility. Christians believe that humans are responsible for looking after everything which actually remains the property of God (and always will). This is Stewardship. Stewardship means looking after something for someone else, something you don't and won't ever own. Christians who see Dominion like this might well be in the front line of a Greenpeace activist event.

Time Out (5)

What evidence is there that humans are harming the environment? How are some humans trying to put that right? Why do some people care about nature and others don't seem to?

Orthodox view

In Genesis the Adamic priesthood for creation is that of an active steward. Humans are called to work with and not against nature so that we can remain worthy of this fragile blue jewel in the cosmic sea, the earth. Our world is not passive in all of this. If we disfigure her, she will reject us and make our life hard and miserable. This will be God's judgement for our abject failure to act as good stewards of HIS creation.

Source: http://www.orthodox.clara.net/stewards_of_creation.htm

Out of condition?

Why does any of this matter to Christians today? Surely the point is to get on with life and live it to the fullest? Christians would say that the Human Condition depends very heavily upon how we find ourselves. What we are is linked with where we're from, how we came to be and what we're here for. The Human Condition depends upon our view of ourselves, but also the intentions God has for us in our lives and in the great plan.

Talking Point 5

'Humans are born good and then learn to be bad.' What do you think?

Activities

Knowledge, Understanding, Evaluation

1 What do Christians think of the idea that God *had* to make humans?

2 What does *ex nihilo* mean?

3 What criticisms could be made of the idea of *ex nihilo*? How would a Christian respond?

4 As well as creating matter, what two other things did God make at the start of the Universe?

5 What problems does the creation of these three things raise?

6 According to the Roman Catholic view on page 11, why did God create humans?

7 In what ways are the workings of the Universe as important to you as how computers work?

8 Why did Mervin the magician's audiences start to dwindle?

9 Why do you think people like mysteries? When are people happy/sad about the solving of a mystery?

10 What was the problem with Dr Siegelibuur's actions?

11 Are there some things which humans shouldn't have the power to do or know?

12 What was (is) the 'God of the gaps' theory?

13 In your own words, describe the first cause argument.

14 State two criticisms of the First Cause Argument.

15 Do you think the First Cause Argument is an effective explanation for the existence of God?

16 According to the Roman Catholic view on page 13, how does the existence of the soul challenge evolution?

17 What difference would it make to people's lives if we could prove that the soul exists?

18 What is the Argument from Design?

19 How effective is the Argument from Design in your opinion?

20 State one criticism of the Argument from Design which you agree with.

21 What does the fact that God made humans last suggest?

22 What things about humans suggest that they were created by a God? What seems to contradict this belief?

23 Explain the three possible meanings of Dominion.

24 Which understanding of Dominion might lead to someone becoming a member of Greenpeace?

25 Which of the understandings of Dominion do you think is most reasonable? Explain your answer.

26 According to the Orthodox view on page 17, what will be the result of human abuse of nature?

27 Should people only treat something well to get something in return?

28 Why do Christians think it is important to think about the human condition?

Practical Activities

1 You read this letter in a newspaper. Reply to it as if you were a Christian.

Dear Sir
The Christians are at it again. God made people. Ha! You only have to look at what people get up to these days to see what a silly idea that is. If God did make them, then isn't it about time he realized his mistake and started again, just like he did with the dinosaurs?
Yours sincerely,
A. Theist

2 In your class, prepare a display board: 'Things I would like to ask God'.

3 Prepare another display board showing images/artwork which support or reject the idea that humans are God's greatest achievement.

4 An environmental organisation wants to design a leaflet encouraging Christians to join its work in saving the planet. Because you know so much about Christianity, they have asked your advice. Design the leaflet.

5 Write a piece of poetry which explores the good/bad side of human beings.

Unit Assessment Question

I1 What would a Christian understand by the phrase '*ex nihilo*'? (2KU)

I2 What responsibilities does a Christian have to the world if God made it? (2KU, 4AE)

Higher
What different things might a Christian mean by the idea of Dominion? (6)

Sample Exam Question

I1 'Dominion is not a blessing, it's a curse'. How might a Christian reply to this statement? (3AE)

I2 According to Christians, why does there need to be a first cause? (4AE)

Higher
What do Christians mean when they describe human beings as 'God's Stewards'? (KU 4)

Homework

Answer the following question in as few words as possible. Perhaps your teacher could arrange a prize for the response with the fewest words (which answers the question).

Why did God create humans?

Personal Reflection

If God did make human beings what difference might it make to your life?

God's Relationship with Humans

God seeking humans for friendship, maybe more. Needs GSOH and no nasty personal habits. Willing to love and serve a creator and in return will receive eternal life and associated benefits. God also offers in return understanding of the meaning of life as well as true personal fulfillment. Replies in prayer to God Direct or email God.com@heaven.org. No details necessary as God knows everything anyway (yes, even that).

Time Out　6

Sit and think about this one – don't write anything down! If God knows everything there is to know about you, what are you currently most happy with yourself about? What are you most ashamed about?

God seeking human

God made humans to enter into a relationship with him. What in the Universe does this mean? Remember God could have chosen not to make anything, but he didn't. He could have chosen not to make any life but he didn't. He could have chosen not to make free-thinking humans but he didn't. Why?

Christians believe that God decided to make humans as the last and greatest of his creations – so this must point to a very special role for humanity.

According to Christian teaching, mankind is made to worship God and to have a relationship with him. Why would God want this? God could have created beings which were forced to love him and associate themselves with him. That would have been easy. But how satisfying is it when you know that someone has no choice but to be your friend. It's much better when the person has chosen this for themselves. This was God's plan: create a being which had the ability to choose to accept God or not (one with free will and the understanding to know about the consequences of its actions). Then . . . let it make its own mind up. But surely humans are a poor choice if they're just flesh and blood – just another animal? Probably. So God did something a little different with humans. He made them in his own image.

This idea, known as the Imago Dei can be understood in different ways: Some think that it means that humans look like God. Others that our personalities are God-like. One common Christian view is that 'in the image of God' means something more. Some have called it the spark of the Divine. This means that God gave to humans some of his own qualities; the ability to reason, love, think, understand and so on. Perhaps it refers to the ability humans have to have relationships with others as well as be aware of a spiritual dimension to life. Whatever it means it is very special – something only humans possess. This quality gives a great deal of power to humans, but it also gives a great deal of responsibility. Humans were made able to have a relationship with God. To choose him or to choose to make themselves Gods instead. Perhaps humans are the only things in the Universe who have the ability to receive God's wavelengths – now there's a responsibility. If this is true then it means something very significant. Remember, God didn't need anything, but Christian teaching states that he chose

to do the things he did, including giving humans their special qualities. Humans have a meaning and a purpose in life, a special job to do. Perhaps it is the unique job of humankind to make all creation aware of its creator. Maybe that's the meaning of life.

Protestant Christian view

To be made in God's image means that man is made to rule just as God rules. Just as God is King over all, man is made to be king over God's creatures on earth. So while mankind is given Dominion and rule, mankind has been given delegated authority under God himself. It is important to understand this if we are to know our role in God's world. Rulership requires great wisdom and responsibility.

Source: http://www.bible-school.co.uk/image-of-god.htm

Getting personal with God

You'd think that being the creator of all things, God wouldn't have much time to get up close and personal. A being of such unimaginable power surely couldn't drop by for tea. But Christians believe he can. Although in a sense, God is beyond the created order of things – outside of space and time – Christians believe that he is personally present in the Universe too and can be personally present in someone's life if that's what they want. This idea is called the Immanence of God. It means that it is possible for everyone to have a personal relationship with God. A God who is impersonal and above it all is not the Christian God, who, Christians believe, is actively present in their everyday lives. People often wonder if a God can possibly be interested in the little things of life. Christians believe that he is. This means that things like prayer make sense, because God is involved in people's lives and cares what happens to them.

Talking Point 7

Have you ever prayed? Has anyone you know ever prayed? Is there any point to prayer? Why might some people reject the idea of prayer?

God might not always think that what we want is right for us, but that's the way things are and doesn't mean that he's not interested. This relationship is two way – like any relationship – you get things out of it but you have to give things too. Christians believe that we need God in our lives to make us complete. Of course God doesn't need anything from us – he just chooses to get involved with us of his own free will.

Time Out 8

Think of a relationship you currently have. In this relationship what do you expect to get out of it? What are you expected to give as part of this relationship?

Orthodox view

God created man and gave him the ability of communion with the Creator via the uncreated divine grace, i.e. via the life-creating energy of the Holy Spirit. In this environment of divine love, man had the ability to cultivate the communion, developing a free and unselfish love towards God and his neighbour.

Therefore man himself should have reached perfection, staying of his own free will in the environment of God, always though having the ability to deny the perfection should he wish to do so.

Source: http://www.eastern-orthodoxy.com/orthodoxy2.htm

Faith again

For many people this is one of the problems with God. If God is there and involved in our lives, why does he not do more to help people? Human life can be hard sometimes – so it seems as if God is remote and disinterested. Earthquakes, violence, hunger all seem to make belief in God difficult. Christians believe that isn't so. God cares and God is with you all the time. It's just a question of faith … again. Sometimes what we might think is good for us isn't, but as humans that's not possible to know – Christians believe God knows.

Silly Example

Elmo wanted to win the lottery. One day he did (on a rollover too). All his dreams would now come true. But he blew it all on fast cars, drinking and pointless holidays. People took advantage of him everywhere and his only 'friends' were those who were after his money. Before he knew it he was very poor and even in heavy debt (to some very dodgy characters). He ended up on the street selling those wee sticky men which crawl down windows when you throw them. He'll never try to win the lottery again. He thought being rich would be everything. How wrong he was. How could he have known?

Christians believe that the human/God relationship is like this. Maybe the things that we want aren't the best things for us at all – but we couldn't know that. So God only gives us what's good for us. This applies particularly to what's called natural evil. These are things which have no human cause, but cause harm and sometimes even death. Why would God let these things happen if he's part of our lives?

Talking Point ⑧

What would be good and bad about winning millions in the lottery? How would your life improve? Might anything in your life get worse?

Another really quite annoying argument for Christians

This is known as the problem of evil and might be a strong attack on Christian beliefs. Bad things happen – God doesn't stop them so he must be weak or bad himself. Christians don't think he's either. They believe that once you've set up a system you have to go with it because otherwise nothing makes any sense. God made the laws of the Universe. These laws sometimes lead to bad things happening. He can't just go about changing the laws when he feels like it. That would be a very unpredictable world – probably impossible to live in

Time Out 9

People drive cars every day even though car accidents are one of the major causes of death in the western world. What other risks do people take in their daily lives? Why?

at all. This means that some bad things are just part of the system. You can't take them away without taking away the good things too. Christians might say that a lot of the things we call natural evil could be avoided if we used our God-given brains. For example, you can't really complain about the effects of a volcanic eruption if you choose to live on a volcano – knowing what volcanoes can do.

Human free will

The other kind of nastiness in the world is the stuff that's caused by people. This can be mass murder or an unkind word to someone. Why does God let this happen? Christians believe that right at the creation of mankind, God made a decision. He gave humans free will. They were allowed to make their own choices in life. They could even reject God if they wanted to. Christians believe that God gave this freedom as the supreme act of love, so freedom is a gift from God. If he'd not given us that then we'd all be robo-people

WE'RE NOT PLAYING WITH YOU!

doing whatever he told us to. This wasn't the kind of humanity God really wanted even though he could have made us that way. He freely chose to make us free and hoped that we'd freely choose him. The trouble with free will is ... well it's free. Free will means that you can choose to do good or evil and God lets you, because otherwise you're not free. Christians believe that God would prefer us to make the right choices but refuses to allow himself to force us to. This means that sometimes we do bad things, but that's unfortunately the price of freedom. To stop us doing the bad things, God would have to take away all our freedom. Christians would argue that if we all lived the life God intended us to then we would always make good choices and so there would be no evil caused by people.

But how do we know what's good or bad?

Talking Point 9

Human freedom is a very important idea in Christian belief, but having this freedom means that bad things are inevitable. Is human freedom that important? What do you think?

Roman Catholic view

Not only the world, however, but also *man himself* has been *entrusted to his own care and responsibility*. God left man 'in the power of his own counsel' (*Sir* 15:14), that he might seek his Creator and freely attain perfection. Attaining such perfection means *personally building up that perfection in himself*. Indeed, just as man in exercising his Dominion over the world shapes it in accordance with his own intelligence and will, so too in performing morally good acts, man strengthens, develops and consolidates within himself his likeness to God.

Source: Pope John Paul II in Veritatis Splendor 1993 Ch 38

Moral conscience

Christians believe that God gave humans a conscience along with free will. This conscience is a voice inside you which guides you when deciding right from wrong. Your conscience doesn't just happen – it builds up with experience over the years and comes from more than one place. A Christian would say that your conscience can grow by:

◆ Listening to God. God speaks directly to people – giving advice. You just have to listen. Sometimes the advice is given more subtly like in a sign or through someone else or by reading something. Some Christians have a tradition of thinking about a decision then opening a Bible at random and choosing a section for guidance. God may speak to you in answer to prayer – or even in your dreams. Sometimes it's just a feeling that you should do something instead of something else.

◆ Listening to others. Your parents, friends, heroes, role models. They all help you to work out right from wrong.

◆ Experience. Sometimes just going through something helps you work out what to do in any similar situation later on.

Christians sometimes speak of the 'still small voice' of God which quietly niggles away at you showing you what's right. When people do wrong all that they have done is refused to listen to what their own moral conscience is telling them.

Apart from this, you don't have to make your morals up for yourself, things have already been done for you. Christians believe that what's right and wrong have already been taught throughout the ages. The Bible is full of teaching about what is right to do and what isn't. As this is the word of God we can take it that it's what God wants from us. God has also sent people to earth to remind us of the difference between right and wrong. Jesus, most obviously, but also saints and holy men and women, priests, ministers, teachers, friends – it could be anyone. God's representatives on Earth, in the form of the Christian Church, also has a long history of trying to teach people right from wrong. Sometimes its got a bit muddled itself, but through its traditions, teachings and examples it tries to make choosing what's right easier.

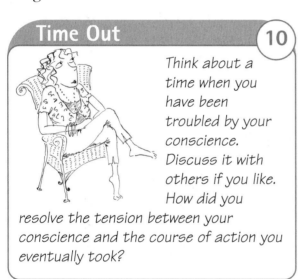

Time Out (10)

Think about a time when you have been troubled by your conscience. Discuss it with others if you like. How did you resolve the tension between your conscience and the course of action you eventually took?

Choices, choices

So God makes humans to a very special recipe. He makes them the only ones who he can have a proper relationship with. He makes them aware of himself and how they can be complete by getting friendly with him by their own choice. But he does let them choose. And there's the problem.

Evangelical Christian view

The bible teaches that when man was first made (created) by God, the relationship between man and God was perfect. We were given a perfect environment in which to live and had a great friendship with the creator of the Universe. All we had to do was choose to stay in the relationship with God. We choose not to stay in that relationship but to break the trust we had. This is the meaning of the first few chapters of Genesis.

Source: http://www.sseconline.com/WhatWeBelieve.html

Activities

Knowledge, Understanding, Evaluation

1 Why did God make humans?

2 Can you force someone to be your friend?

3 What different understandings are there of the concept of Imago Dei?

4 If humans are special, what powers does this give us/what responsibilities?

5 Why might God have wanted to have a relationship with another being?

6 Do you think humans were a good choice?

7 According to the Protestant view on page 22, what does it mean to be made in God's image?

8 What is meant by the Immanence of God?

9 How does the Immanence of God make prayer worthwhile?

10 Why do Christians believe that God will not give us everything we ask for?

11 According to the Orthodox view on page 23, what did God give humans?

12 Why might it seem as if God is sometimes disinterested in human life?

13 Do you think Elmo on page 24 should never have won the lottery?

14 What is the difference between natural and human-caused evil?

15 Why do both present a challenge for Christians?

16 How would a Christian explain why God 'allows' natural evil?

17 Explain, in your own words, the free-will argument.

18 Do you think freedom is more important than anything else? Explain your answer.

19 According to the Roman Catholic view on page 26, how can humans strengthen their likeness to God?

20 What is meant by moral conscience?

21 What kinds of things affect the development of moral conscience?

22 State two specifically Christian ways of working out what's right and wrong.

23 According to the Evangelical Christian view on this page, how could humans have lived in a perfect environment?

Practical Activities

1 Reply to the personal ad from God (see page 20) on behalf of all human beings – what do you think humans have to offer God?

2 Draw up a contract between God and mankind. On one side write what you think God should contribute to the relationship and on the other what humans should contribute. Think about what would have to happen to break this contract.

3 Some people think that even in the world's worst natural disasters, there is evidence of the work of a loving God. Do some research into this and set up a display suggesting how good things can sometimes come out of bad.

4 Imagine you were given everything in life you ever wanted. How would you feel? What would you do next? Write an imaginative story based on this idea.

5 Get people in your class to anonymously write a short paragraph about their conscience completing the two statements below. You could pass these round the room with people's permission or display them – but make sure they are unidentifiable.

◆ Something I have on my conscience is . . .

◆ One time when my conscience stopped me from doing something was . . .

6 Look into the life of someone who kept up a relationship with God through their faith (e.g. Martin Luther King/Mother Teresa etc.) Make this into a short project about Christians who lived by faith.

Unit Assessment Question

I1 State one way in which a Christian decides what is right and wrong. (2KU)

I2 Why is it important for Christians that humans have free will? (2KU, 4AE)

Higher
'God chose to give humans free will. This was a mistake.' How far would a Christian agree? (8)

Sample Exam Question

I1 In the creation story, what is meant by 'in the image of God'? (2KU)

I2 State one reason a Christian might give to answer the question 'Why did God create humans?' (2KU)

Higher
What do Christians mean when they say that humans are 'created in the image of God'? (4 KU, 4 AE)

Homework

Think through your life as it is now. What things are you free to do and what things are you not free to do that you would like to?

Personal Reflection

Do you think guilt is a helpful emotion or not? Explain your answer.

Sin and The Fall

Come on, will you? Give me a break. It was just one wee bite. I couldn't really say no could I? You made her for me after all, my ribs are still sore. She's a total babe too. How am I supposed to just ignore her when she asks me, you know ... like that ...?

'Just one wee crunch' say she. 'It's dead nice ... really juicy and sweet ... not exactly going to kill you is it?'

Well, I figured you weren't about – so where's the harm? Just to try it, then I'll give it up – not like I'm going to get a habit nor nothin'. Just once, just to see. Anyway, what's the big deal in the first place? It's just a tree. And another thing – was it not a wee bit of a tease? I didny think you could really be all that serious about it. I mean to say, just telling us *not to* really made us *want to* – you know what I mean?

I remember your exact words ... well pretty much anyway ...

See this whole garden. It's for you. Both of you can eat anything you want in it . . . well nearly anything. There's just this one wee tree I want you to stay away from . . . no, don't ask why. Just keep your nebs out of that one . . . Right?

Well, I thought you were having us on so I did. So I had one wee nibble of that apple. I know you told us not to, but, well, I . . . well it's not the end of the world exactly is it? Then does all hell no break loose – if you'll excuse the pun in the circumstances . . . I didny know I was starkers – man, they fig leaves are itchy eh? Well maybe you wouldny know . . .

Is, eh, beggin your pardon, chucking us oot the garden not just a wee bit over-reacting? And, what is 'work' while we're on the topic anyway – sounds a bit nippy to me. And as for this 'childbirth' business, that sounds a wee bit gross if you don't mind me saying so . . .

Anyway it wasn't me, it was her. OK, it wasn't just her – it was that snake. Come to think of it, your snake . . . Alright, alright, I get your point . . .

Time Out

 (11)

Read the story upon which this is based in Genesis 1. Make your own summary of the order of the events in the story. If you are artistic you could do this in the form of illustrations.

Original sin

Maybe there's nothing very original about sin as far as you're concerned! Sin seems like quite an old-fashioned word for many people. Something your great Granny might talk about. The story you have just read is a Christian explanation to answer the question 'Where did Sin come from?'. Christians believe that Sin is when we do something wrong. It's when we

don't live up to the things we really should do. For Christians, there's an extra ingredient in the Sin recipe:

Sin is when we choose to go our own way instead of the way God wants us to go.

Christians believe that this happened first with Adam and Eve. God told them not to eat from a certain tree. They disobeyed God and hey presto – sin sneaks in through the back door. Adam and Eve set a pattern which all humans would follow afterwards. Their sin is

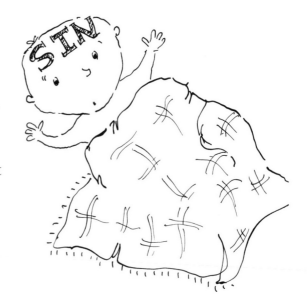

passed on to us – so that we're born with it. This just means that it's now human nature to sin. Sin is like a stain on our character which needs to be washed away, but it's a pretty stubborn stain. For thousands of years, women got the blame for the actions of Eve – as if Adam was just some poor sad soul who did what Eve told him without thinking. Nowadays, Christians tend to think that both of them were to blame – but wait a minute …

Roman Catholic view

'We believe that in Adam all have sinned. By that we mean that the original sin he committed affected human nature itself. In what way? Through his sin, human nature, common to all men, fell into a state in which it incurs the consequences of his act. This new state, then, is not the one in which human nature first existed in our First Parents. They, in their origin, were set up by God in a state of holiness and righteousness. They had no experience of evil or of sin. But it is their fallen nature which has been passed on to all their descendants'.

Pope Paul VI in his Credo of the People of God (1968) Section 16

Talking Point 10

What is a sin? When did you last sin? Have you ever felt guilty?

Do you Adam and Eve it?

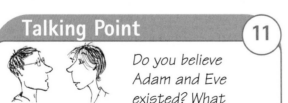

Talking Point 11

Do you believe Adam and Eve existed? What reasons do you have for your beliefs? What do others in your class think? What arguments are given in favour of/against their existence?

Was there an Adam and Eve? Did this story happen? What does it all mean?

For people who aren't Christians, the Adam and Eve story might seem a bit far-fetched. It sounds very much like a fairy tale, and a pretty odd explanation of why humans and God don't get on together the way they should. It leads to all sorts of questions like:

> Where did Adam and Eve's children get their husbands and wives?

> Why give them a free choice then punish them for the choice they made?

> Why did God let the snake tempt them in the first place?

> Why blame us all for the mistakes of two people?

If you accept that the Adam and Eve story is true, then maybe it raises more questions than it answers. If you don't accept that it's true, then why should anything else in the Bible be true? Some people think that the Adam and Eve story doesn't make sense, so it's false, therefore the Bible is false – therefore Christianity isn't worth giving any time to, therefore you might as well do as you please. For lots of people it is an 'either/or' situation. Either Adam and Eve were real or they weren't. If they weren't, then Christianity collapses on page one. But obviously millions of Christians have got onto page two without too much trouble. How do they explain Adam and Eve?

Time Out 12

Everyone in your class should write their own personal response to the Adam and Eve story – anonymously. These should be displayed in class and discussed.

All perfectly true

Why is it any more likely that Adam and Eve didn't exist than that they did? Yes, no-one was there to prove that they existed – but that means no-one was there to prove they didn't either. Did your great great great great great great Grandmother exist? When was she born? What was her name? What colour hair did she have? You don't know? Tut tut. But did she exist? She must have done or where did you come from? But can you *prove* it? Probably not in most cases (maybe you were left by aliens). Believing in Adam and Eve is an act of faith. There's nothing to say that

I did exist!

the story about them is false. It is strange, but so what? Christians could argue that the story was given to the writers of the Bible by God – so it is what happened. Or, the story could have been passed by Adam and Eve to their children who passed it to their children and so on down the ages. So, there's no reason to doubt the story when you come right down to it.

Bible Theology Ministries' view

Adam and Eve were literal people and literally a pair, man and woman. They were literally the first people on earth, from whom all other peoples throughout history descended. Adam was literally made of clay. Eve was literally made of one of Adam's rib bones. When created, Adam and Eve were perfect in every sense. When they sinned they brought death and destruction upon the whole of humanity and a curse upon the rest of Creation.

Source: http://www.christiandoctrine.net/about/beliefs_web.htm#1.%20Creation

True in a way

There was an Adam and Eve, but the story is a simple way of explaining a complicated problem. God made humans, humans chose to ignore him, God punished them for that. The story is just a piece of drama to explain a difficult idea. There wasn't really a tree or a fruit – these are just metaphors of something else entirely – they stand for other things. Like the following:

Thing in the Story . . .	Stands for . . .
Adam and Eve	All humankind
The Tree	The source of good and evil
The Fruit	The choice between God and self
The Serpent	The habit of humans to think they know best

. . . and so on. Stories help us to get mental pictures, remember things more easily and understand things more completely. Adam and Eve is a story for grown-ups to answer the question 'Why have God and mankind fallen out?'.

Time Out (13)

Copy and complete this table above. Extend the table by adding your own ideas, giving as many explanations as you can for each element of the story. You'll have to read the story in the Bible first and make a list of all the elements and then think about what they might mean.

Talking Point (12)

When have you been helped to understand something through a story?

Not an issue

Some Christians feel that stories like Adam and Eve aren't something we should get worked up about. You don't have to accept every single word in the Bible as literally true. It didn't all need to happen the way it is written. There are some exaggerations in there, some fancy stories to get a point across. Just because you think Adam and Eve is only a story doesn't make you a failed Christian. The Bible was written long ago, for people who were very different from people in the 21st Century. It used ideas and language which people long ago would have understood. It told stories just like other writings from other lands and cultures nearby. The message in the story is true even if the events didn't actually happen. People today still choose to go their own way – 'to eat from whatever tree they choose'. All religions mix story with fact – just accept it, and get onto what's important – what it all means.

WE'RE NOT PLAYING WITH YOU!

The meaning of the story

◆ Humankind made by God

◆ Life with God is easy

◆ Life without God is hard

◆ Humans are given the free choice to follow God or live without him

◆ Humans choose to live without him

◆ Choosing to live without God makes life hard

◆ Sin = choosing to live without God

◆ Results of sin = life is harder

Time Out (14)

In no less than 75 words and in your own words, explain how a Christian might understand the story of Adam and Eve.

Time Out (15)

Complete the following with as many statements as you can.

Human nature is . . .

Can sin, Will sin . . .?

So Christians believe that when we are separated from God, we will make bad choices leading to sin. This isn't just because we're not listening to God's helpful advice about what is right to do, but because: When humans live without God we make ourselves God. Having no-one to answer to but ourselves – we can do anything. If this view is right, then it means that sinning is just part of being human – it's part of our nature. People are bound to sin . . . pun intended.

Methodist view

> The created order is designed for the well-being of all creatures and as the place of human dwelling in covenant with God. As sinful creatures, however, we have broken that covenant, become estranged from God, wounded ourselves and one another, and wreaked havoc throughout the natural order. We stand in need of redemption.

Source: http://www.gbgm-umc.org/weidman/UMBELIEFS.html

The effects of sin

Obvious really, but here we go:

◆ Sin separates God and humanity. God made humans with the intention that they obeyed and got into a relationship with him. Humans disobeyed so God and man fell out – hence the Adam and Eve story is sometimes known as The Fall. Continuing to sin keeps us apart from God. This falling out with God is called alienation.

◆ If God and humanity were pals, then life for us would be easy just like it was in Eden. After The Fall, life became full of hardships and remains so today. Humans were meant to be in a relationship with God – without that we can't be all we can be.

◆ Sinning harms the sinner. When we do wrong there are sometimes consequences for us here and now. But there are also consequences in the future. Keeping sinning keeps us apart from God – we might die and remain separated from God for all eternity. For Christians, this is a fairly gruesome thought.

◆ Sinning harms others. When we do wrong there are consequences for others. Our bad actions have consequences – sometimes harming perfectly innocent people.

◆ Sin also has consequences for all creation. When Adam sinned all creation paid the price of being separated from God. Humans became not only alienated from God but from everything else in creation too. Remember humans were given a special role by God. Through sin they gave up that role.

◆ When sin came into the world it brought two unpleasant pals. Death came into the world and so did suffering. Without sin we wouldn't have to be bothered by these at all.

Talking Point 13

Do you think the Christian view of humans as sinners is a depressing one? Discuss in class and note any interesting views expressed.

Talking Point 14

'God gave humans free will and then got angry with their free choice. This shows that God's a bit mixed up.' What do you think?

Freedom to sin

Christians argue that humans misuse our God-given free will, and that's one of the major problems of the human condition. We know what we should do, we know how to do it, we just don't always choose to do it. Sin is caused by exercising our free will in the wrong way – just like Adam did. But, if God lets us freely choose, why should he get angry when we don't choose what he wants us to choose? God did. When Adam and Eve were given the choice they chose to disobey God and were punished – is that fair? Christians believe it is.

Every choice we have has consequences (that's what our moral conscience helps us with) so a bad choice leads to bad consequences. It's a simple equation really, and we can't say we weren't warned!

Jesus saves

Of course, Christians believe that God has given us some pretty obvious hints about how to avoid sinning. Most obviously in the person of Jesus. But they also believe that Jesus was the most important way in which God tried to sort out the alienation caused by The Fall. Christians believe that Jesus came to turn Adam's decision around and put it right. Jesus is even called the new Adam. In fact, Jesus putting right Adam's wrong was so important that it explains why Jesus had to be completely human (more of that later).

Christians believe:

Now these are fairly hefty statements, regularly uttered in churches – but what do they mean? Some might say that ordinary everyday Christians might feel that these statements are like answers in Higher English, 'I know what it means, but it's hard to explain'. So let's try.

'Jesus died for our sins' – Humans should really be punished for all the rotten things that we do, but God treats humans like a loving parent would. He is endlessly patient and forgiving. In fact, so forgiving that instead of punishing us for our sins he sent his only son to take the punishment for us. He stands in for us and takes the knocks that we deserve. It's our sin that led to Jesus' suffering and death, and that's a not-so-subtle hint that our free choices can lead to hardships for others – including those who really don't deserve it.

'Jesus died to rescue us from sin' – Sin clings to you like a bad smell – remember how guilty you felt for how long after the last really horrible thing you did. Sin eats you up – it feeds itself by making one sin lead to another – Jesus came to break this vicious circle by showing us a better way.

'Jesus came to take away our sins' – So Jesus took our sins on himself and took them off our shoulders. In Old Testament times a goat would be symbolically given the sins of a community and sent into the desert to die – it became the scapegoat. Jesus was the scapegoat for everyone.

'Jesus paid the price of sin' – There's a cost to sin. It keeps humans and God apart, so it spoils the relationship between creator and created – it also causes harm to the sinner and the sinned against. In short, it's really not very nice. The price of this sin was as high as you can get. The death of your only son. Christians believe that God's love for mankind is so great, and his desire to get the relationship right with his creation is so strong that he was willing to put his son through some pretty nasty stuff to pay off the sin debt.

> ## Talking Point (15)
>
>
>
> *'Jesus was God. God killed himself to pay himself to buy us out of sin'. Does this make sense? How do Christians explain this?*

'Jesus showed us the way to escape sin' – Now this part has a number of elements:

◆ If God loved us that much, then he must be worth getting friendly with again. So give up the sinning and follow him. Jesus' death was the most powerful wake-up call you can imagine.

◆ Jesus showed that accepting the will of God – i.e. putting God's will before your own – was the right way. By doing this he beat death and lives for ever beside God. If humans do God's will, not their own, then they can achieve the same thing.

◆ The example of Jesus' life shows how to freely choose the right thing all the time – and so do what God wants. There are no secrets about how to behave.

The life and teaching of Jesus show us the way to live sin-free lives. Christians believe that Jesus lived a sin-free life. He's the role model to follow.

Orthodox view

We believe that God has got involved personally in the affairs of this world to save mankind.

He did not merely lecture us from afar, blame us or teach us how to try and accept things as they are. He came down to earth to sort the problems out.

He left us not simply the example and teaching of His Son's life but also the way into a newness of life, through the death-defeating resurrection of Christ.

When Christ ascended to heaven, the Father sent unto us the Holy Spirit to continue this salvation work. God has never left us alone to suffer the consequences of our own stupidity and weakness, our waywardness and rebellion. Like any true and loving Father he has and still does get involved. We, as his followers, can do no less.

Source: http://www.orthodox.clara.net/god_gets_involved.htm

Time Out 16

What evidence is there of God intervening in people's everyday lives? Should God get involved?

So why is avoiding sin so difficult?

Christians believe that we're born with original sin. So it's in our nature and we have to work hard to overcome our nature. Being good is actually quite tricky sometimes – it's much easier just to do what we want, whatever the consequences. Sometimes we make decisions without really thinking about what the consequences might be. Besides, many people will argue that the rewards for being good aren't always obvious – and to wait until you die for your reward in heaven just doesn't make sense. We live in a world where people want proof for everything – to say that you should avoid sin so that you can overcome death needs a high level of faith. There's no proof of an afterlife – so why live your whole life because of it?

While some Christians think that sinning is just self-motivated free choice, others think that the Serpent which tempted Eve is still around in the form of the Devil. It's the Devil who sneakily persuades you to sin – we don't really need much pushing and the Devil's quite 'good' at pushing us in dodgy directions. Some Christians think of the Devil as a real person, others as some kind of evil force. Others think the Devil is just a way of explaining the human tendency to want to do bad things.

Carry out a survey in your school about belief in the Devil. Do people believe in such a being? What images do people have of the Devil? How does this compare with people's views of God?

Talking Point 16

If there is a Devil, why does God let him do his dodgy work? Why doesn't God just squash him?

Another problem is just how 'free' we actually are. Some say that free will is a bit of an illusion – we are a product of our experiences, our upbringing, where we live, what kind of DNA we have. Choosing to do the right thing is less easy if you've had a troubled upbringing than if you haven't. What if we could find a gene which makes people murderers – should we remove it? If people sin because of things outside their control, then how can we be 'blamed' for sin? This is the opposite of free will and is called Determinism.

In fact, this takes us right back to one of the big problems of the Adam and Eve story. If it is in human nature to sin, and God designed human nature, then doesn't God share some of the blame for sin? Also, if God lets the Devil run amok in the world today, encouraging our sinful ways, is that really fair – especially as we can't see him and so cannot fight back?

Time Out 18

What things in your life influence your behaviour and moral choices?

Or is sin something which is all our own fault and something we have to fight against – even if it is in our nature? Is it just an unavoidable part of the human condition?

More importantly perhaps, are we just doomed to sin and suffer its consequences?

Activities

Knowledge, Understanding, Evaluation

1 In your own words, describe the events surrounding the fall of Adam in Genesis.

2 What do Christians mean by sin?

3 According to the Roman Catholic view on page 33, what is original sin?

4 What problems might the existence of an actual Adam and Eve pose for Christians?

5 State two different ways in which Christians understand the Adam and Eve story.

6 How important do you think it is for Christians to believe that Adam and Eve actually existed?

7 What view does the Bible Theology Ministries have about Adam and Eve?

8 State two of the features of the Adam and Eve story and show how they could be understood metaphorically.

9 What, for Christians, is the message in the Adam and Eve story?

10 Do you agree that sinning is just part of human nature? What evidence do you have to support your views?

11 According to the Methodist view on page 37, what has sin meant for our relationship with God?

12 In your own words, state three of the effects of sin.

13 God got angry with Adam's free choice. How do Christians explain this anger?

14 What do Christians mean when they call Jesus the 'New Adam'?

15 What does it mean to say that Jesus took the punishment for human sin?

16 Why do Christians think that God's sending Jesus was a supreme act of love towards humans?

17 According to the Orthodox view on page 41, how does God show that he is a 'loving father'?

18 What different views do Christians have about the Devil?

19 How far do you think the Devil is a good explanation for the existence of evil?

20 Do you think humans can't help their nature? What evidence is there of humans overcoming what seems to be 'human nature'?

21 How would a Christian defend the belief that God is to blame for 'human nature'?

Practical Activities

1 Tell the story of The Fall in your own way. You could do this as a class drama or as your own version of the story in a humorous way. Perhaps you could write it in rhyming verse or like a TV soap. You could use characters from already existing TV shows to do this – or even do it in the form of a pantomime script.

2 Design a piece of artwork entitled 'Sin'. A collage of images might work here – have a look at paintings by people like Salvador Dali or Hieronymous Bosch for ideas.

3 See if you can find any stories from your family's past which are surprising – maybe your great great great great Grandmother's life story was even more strange than the Adam and Eve story!

4 Turn the events and meaning of The Fall into a matching game. Write the events on one set of cards and the meanings on another. (See also the textual work in section 5.) Now turn them all face down on a table and then turn over two at a time until you have a matching pair.

5 In a group, take one of the six bullet points about the effects of sin on pages 37–38. Now illustrate this effect in artwork.

6 Using the information in the section 'Jesus Saves' on page 39, make up a crossword and pass it to others in your class to do.

Unit Assessment Question

I1 State one way a Christian would think Jesus showed us how to escape sin. (2KU)

I2 What would a Christian mean by saying that 'Jesus died for our sins'? (4KU)

Higher
Explain two ways in which Christians think Jesus saves people from sin. (8)

Sample Exam Question

I1 State one possible effect of sin. (2KU)

I2 What does a Christian understand by sin? (2KU)

Higher
According to Christians, how did sin come into the world and what are its effects (8 KU)

Homework

Write a 100 word answer to the following question after discussion with other people. Perhaps some discussion with your parents might be interesting to have (!).

'Is the idea of sin out of date?'

Personal Reflection

Christians believe that the world's problems are a result of our alienation from God. What do you think?

Forgiveness and Salvation

The Prodigal Son

A rich farmer had two sons,
A hard-working and a slobby one.
The slob one day said 'I hate being stuck
With farms and smells and all this muck
Why do I have to live this way,
Dad, give me money and I'll go away.'
'But son', said Dad, 'You'll get your gold
When I'm dead and gone and laid out cold'.
'But by that time I might be done
Give me money now while I can still have fun'.
So Dad gave him his due finance
Every penny of his inheritance –
Off slob son went to spend it all
He would be sure to have a ball.
Hard-working son still laboured and toiled
Though seeing his brother yet again spoiled
While slob son went to every place
Where folks were glad to see his face.
Without a care he spent and spent
Blowing it all wherever he went
'Til one grim day he sadly found
He was right down to his last pound –
He held it tightly in his hand
But slipped and lost it in the sand.
So now with nothing, but still a slob
He knew he'd have to get a job
Horror! Work!
What a Dork.
Eventually he found somewhere,
A boss with very little hair
Who said, 'Now boy here's what you do
You shovel all that nice pig poo'.
No time for slob to sit and think
Working hard all·day despite the stink
But soon he thought 'I'm mad –
I'll just go back to Dad
I'll work for him as a lowly slave
I wasted everything he gave
Scumbag, Waster, that is me
But maybe Dad will take pity'.
So back he went so sheepishly,
But from afar his Dad did see
His only other son appear

In some pretty niffy gear
Looking tired, looking ill
Cos he'd munched so much pigswill.
His father cheered and ran to slob
And hugged and kissed him (but not on the gob)
'I'm a dopey numpty. I've been so bad
I'm not fit to call you Dad'.
But Dad looked full of joy,
'My son! My kid! My brilliant boy!
Bring the best robe for my son to wear
Sandals, for his feet are bare
A ring to put his finger through
And see that fat calf – Barbecue!'
The other son, he heard the commotion
Someone must have got promotion
A servant said "Your brother's here
Your father's full of cheesy cheer
He's killed the calf and ordered a party
And got your brother dressed all tarty".
The working son spat in the dust
And could not contain his true disgust,
'All this time I've done my bit
Worked hard, been good and then that twit
Comes home and it's all hee hee hee
You've never been like that to me'.
'My son' said Dad, 'you need correction,
I've always shown you true affection.
All that's mine is yours as well
But my son I have to tell
My other son has come around
Not dead but alive, not lost but found!'

Compare with Luke 15: 11–32

Time Out 19

Imagine the two brothers meet to talk the next day. How might their conversation go? What might the hard-working brother think about his slobby sibling?

Talking Point 17

'The Dad in the story was quite right to forgive his son.'

What do you think?

Talking Point 18

'Forgiving others is much more difficult but much more powerful than holding a grudge.' What do you think?

Time Out 20

Describe a time when you have had to forgive or be forgiven. Alternatively make a mental list of 'Things I'd like to be forgiven for'.

Forgiving others

Christians stress the power of forgiveness. No matter what you have done, if you ask for forgiveness you can receive it. When someone asks for forgiveness you don't cast up all the grot they've done, you start over again with them. Christians believe that anyone can be forgiven for anything provided that they truly want to be forgiven and very importantly, they promise not to do the things again that they've just been forgiven for. Jesus stopped a woman being stoned to death for having an affair. But at the end of it all he said to her, 'Go and sin no more'. (See John 8:11). Zacchaeus the tax-collector proved that he was sorry for his actions by giving back even more than he stole. Christians believe that God's forgiveness is absolute and free, but not without conditions. The story above is the Parable of the Prodigal Son and is a way of understanding God's forgiveness. Like the father in the story, God forgives when asked because he is so pleased that someone has returned to him. The father does not moan at the slob son for all he's done wrong. Instead he hugs him for what he's now done right! The son has shown an important quality – repentance.

Salvation Army view

What then is repentance? Repentance is simply renouncing sin, turning round from darkness to light, from the power of Satan unto God. This is giving up sin in your heart, in purpose, in desire; resolving that you will give up every evil thing, and that you will do it now. Of course this involves sorrow; for how will any sane man turn himself round from a given course into another if he does not repent? It implies, also, hatred of the course he formerly took, and from which he turns.

Catherine Booth

Grace and works

Once you have repented you will live a good life – what does that do for you? There has been some tension within Christianity about whether eternal life comes through doing good works or through grace. Some Christians may believe that you have to be good to get into heaven or to find favour with God. Others argue that no-one can ever be good enough no matter what we do, but we can

get into heaven or receive eternal life by the grace of God. All this means is that our belief is what gets us our forgiveness. God's grace, like the forgiveness of the father in the story, knows no ends. Forgiveness is based on faith alone. Forgiveness is the first step to Salvation – being saved from your sins. Nowadays many Christians would argue that it's not either/or with grace and works, it's both. They say that God forgives you no matter what, provided that you are sincere when you ask for forgiveness. This is what saves you from sin. But ... you can only really show that you are sincere in asking for forgiveness if you follow it up with a changed life. The Prodigal Son parable is taken by Christians to be a metaphor for the relationship between God and mankind in this way: Like the son, humans want it all on a plate from God – they ask to go their own way. So God lets them, but pretty soon humans discover that it isn't that easy going it alone. The sensible thing to do is to return to God and ask his forgiveness, which he'll gladly give. Being a Christian is like being the slob son. No-one has got it right yet, but return to the Father and all will be forgiven. In fact, more than that – not only will you be forgiven, but you'll be welcomed back with open arms in an attitude of celebration. Not bad, eh?

Talking Point (19)

Some Christians think you have to do good works to get into heaven. What kind of good works do you think they mean?

Christian view

Almost every spiritual path known to man relies on good works to get to its version of heaven. Christianity is the one spiritual path where people need to rely on something completely different: grace. Note that Christianity is still big on doing good, but never for the sake of getting to heaven:

There are three problems with relying on good works to get to heaven.

◆ Good works provide no measure of "good enough";

◆ Good works offer no assurance of making it to heaven;

◆ Good works ask God to turn a blind eye.

Source: http://web.ukonline.co.uk/scotsbaker/faqgoodworks.html

Time Out (21)

Find out about the history of the Jewish religion and then the Christian religion. What evidence is there in both that God has tried to re-establish good relationships with humanity? Prepare a short report on the issue.

Ending alienation ... a long history

Slob son and his Dad were alienated from each other in this story because slob son decided he didn't need his Dad or the life he could offer. Slob son went his own way and then realised his mistake. Christians believe that God has tried hard since Adam's big mistake to put things right with humans – to get them to come back to him where they belong. God made agreements with Abraham and Noah. He delivered his people from slavery in Egypt. He sent prophet after prophet to remind people that he still cared for them. All through the history of the relationship between God and mankind, God has been trying to get the message across that he is still our Father and wants to welcome his children back again. Christians believe that the final act of this was the life and death of Jesus, where God showed that his desire to forgive mankind was so strong that he sent his only son to live and die among us.

Christians believe that Jesus is the last chance to get things right with God. Even on the cross, Jesus was heard to say 'Father, forgive them, for they don't know what they're doing'. This showed not only that Christians should be absolutely forgiving, but also that God forgives us even the act of killing his own flesh and blood. If sin is a bad stain on the character of humanity, Christians believe that it can be washed away by Jesus, by his sacrificial blood. More of that later too.

Christian views

We are accounted righteous before God only for the merit of our Lord and Saviour Jesus Christ, by faith, and not for our own works or deservings. Wherefore, that we are justified by faith, only, is a most wholesome doctrine, and very full of comfort.

Article IX Of the Justification of Man (The Articles of Religion of the Methodist Church, the Discipline of 1808)

Those whom God effectually calls, He also freely justifies; not by infusing righteousness into them, but by pardoning their sins, and by accounting and accepting their persons as righteous; not for any thing wrought in them, or done by them, but for Christ's sake alone; nor by imputing faith itself, the act of believing, or any other evangelical obedience to them, as their righteousness; but by imputing the obedience and satisfaction of Christ unto them, they receiving and resting on Him and His righteousness by faith; which faith they have not of themselves, it is the gift of God.

Chapter XI. Of Justification: Westminster Confession of Faith (1647)

Talking Point (20)

'It is important to accept people just as they are.' What do you think?

Time Out (22)

What evidence is there in the world today that people are 'walking in darkness'?

Saving us from the human condition

So for Christians, the potentially perfect palhood between God and his creation has gone squiffy. This is because mankind chose to ignore God and go his own way. But God doesn't want to give up on mankind and keeps trying to put it right. Humans still have a choice but God still keeps sending the signs to show us the right way. But, it remains our choice – God won't force us to love him or even to think about him. Christians believe that if we choose to reject God then we will continue to walk in darkness (very dangerous and a bit scary). If, however, we choose to accept God then we can walk in the light (much more pleasant and you can see where you're going). It is human nature to sin – but with God's help that human nature can be overcome. Christians believe that we only have to ask.

Activities

Knowledge, Understanding, Evaluation

1 What did the prodigal son want from his father?

2 What do you think his brother would have thought about this and his father's decision to agree to the son's request?

3 How did the prodigal son end up wanting to go back to his father?

4 What do you think about the father's reaction to the return of his son?

5 Was the hard-working brother treated unfairly?

6 What do Christians understand the message of this parable to be?

7 How did Zacchaeus prove that he had repented?

8 What did Jesus ask the woman who was going to be stoned to do to prove that she had repented?

9 What is the link between forgiveness, repentance and salvation?

10 According to Catherine Booth, once you have been forgiven, what are you expected to do?

11 What is the difference between grace and works?

12 When someone asks you for forgiveness, how can you be sure they are truly sorry?

13 According to the Christian view on page 48, what are the problems with good works?

14 What stories in the Old Testament show that God tried to end the alienation between God and mankind?

15 How can sin be like a bad stain?

16 What evidence is there that the Methodist Church believes that faith is more important than good works?

17 What evidence is there that the Westminster Confession of faith agrees?

18 Based on what you have studied so far, why do you think God doesn't just give up trying to get it right with humans?

19 For a Christian, what will accepting God lead to?

Practical Activities

1 Tell the story of the prodigal son in the form of a tabloid newspaper – make it as sensational as possible. Think of a suitable headline and get the human interest angle in!

2 Years later, once the hard-working son has really got to grips with it all, his father writes him a letter explaining his actions. What kinds of things would the father say?

3 Think of a list of things which people do which they might ask forgiveness for. For each one, suggest a possible course of action which might show that the person has truly repented of their wicked ways.

For example: *Thief – return the property and paint the victim's house for free!*

4 Write down as many good works as you can in three minutes (exactly). Who can get most? Do the same by just saying them and getting someone else to count for you.

Unit Assessment Question

I1 In the story of the prodigal son, why might the hard-working son have been angry? (2AE)

I2 'In the story of the prodigal son, the father was right to forgive his son'. Do you agree? Give reasons for your answer. (2KU, 6AE)

Higher
How does the story of the prodigal son illustrate Christian beliefs about forgiveness? (6)

Sample Exam Question

I1 What is meant by repentance? (2KU)

I2 'You can't be forgiven unless you are sorry for your actions'. How might a Christian respond to this statement? (4AE)

Higher
'To become a Christian starts with repentance.' How far would a Christian agree?
(2 KU, 8 E)

Homework

Write the outline for a film of the prodigal son story. Set the film in a modern context and using modern ideas.

Personal Reflection

What would you have done if you'd been the father in the prodigal son story?

Textual Sources

As with all the texts in this course, you should read them in their original form. Remember to use the version of the Bible which the SQA advises, but it's a good idea to look at other versions too. Sometimes the way something is translated in a different version might help you to understand it all better.

Genesis 1: 1–2: 17

This gives an account of the creation of the Universe as well as life on earth. Some Christians accept it as literally true. Others think it is a story or myth, which refers to the truth, but in a simplistic way which makes the story understandable. Other Christians think it is just a story with a message, meant to convey the belief that God made everything for a purpose.

Element of the story	Commentary
God creates the heavens and the earth and life on earth in a set order. These are described as days.	Some Christians point to the structure of the creation as being close to modern views of how the Universe and life on earth developed. The word bara is used for creation, suggesting the making of something which would be impossible for mankind to make. Some Christians believe the days were 24 hours as now, others that this is just a form of expression in the story.
On the sixth day, God makes man.	Man is made in the image of God which most theologians take to mean that mankind is able to have communion with God in a way that other living things are not.
On the seventh day, God rests.	This sets the pattern for the shabat to come – shabat is the Hebrew word for rest.
In 2: 4–3: 24, God takes the name Yahweh Elohim.	God gives his name which has the meaning 'I am who I am' or 'I will be who I will be'. God explains to mankind that who he is can be understood by what he does. This suggests that God will reveal himself throughout history showing the kind of creator he is.

Element of the story	Commentary
Adam is created.	The Hebrew word 'adam' means mankind and the word 'damah' means the soil. Whether he was the very first man or this is just a story about one of the first men is a matter of discussion in Christianity.
The trees of good and evil.	Some Christian theologians suggest that the phrasing of this section suggests that Adam knew what the consequences of disobeying God's request about these trees would be.

Genesis 3: 1–24

This story is sometimes referred to as the fall of Adam. Many Christians believe that it is literally true, others believe that it is a metaphor of the relationship between the first humans and their creator, God. The story contrasts the perfect world of the Garden of Eden – where everything is perfect and life is completely easy with the punishment following The Fall. Put simply before The Fall, life is a paradise, after The Fall, life is hellish. Pain, suffering, toil and death arrive through the actions of The Fall. In the story God safeguards mankind's freedom by asking him not to eat free of the tree, not commanding him. The only issue is why God allowed the serpent to tempt Adam and Eve into disobedience. Would they have fallen without the serpent's influence?

Element of the story	Commentary
Adam and Eve placed in a garden where all is perfect – nothing has to be worked for.	God gives mankind everything they need. Everything is a gift with no strings attached. Humans need only depend on God for everything. In return for obedience God provides everything.
God asks that Adam and Eve do not eat from one particular tree.	This is a request, not an order. Also, God does not physically withhold anything. It's all up to Adam and Eve. Humanity is given free choice. Eating from the tree will demonstrate man's disobedience and that he wants to reject God and all that he offers.
The snake tempts Eve to eat from the tree by suggesting that God must have some reason for asking them not to.	Eve is just following her nature. Humans are curious and it is in their nature to do what they know they shouldn't. Eve realises that the tree means some kind of awareness of what it's like to be God instead of a subject of God. This desire for some kind of power is just too much for her.
After eating the fruit they realise that they are naked.	The fruit is self-awareness which they hadn't had before. Perhaps awareness of your own existence is something which is god-like. The nakedness is their realisation that they are 'exposed' now – they can no longer hide in an ideal world but have to face up to the reality of their choice – that the world is now on their shoulders.

Element of the story	Commentary
They feared their nakedness in the sight of God.	They knew that they would be found out and now knew that actions have consequences. Human nature is something you can't hide – you have to face up to it.
You will now work.	Humans had been given Dominion over the earth. Now even the soil would rebel against them and fight against humans taking things from it. A bit of a humiliation. With God everything is easy. Without him, everything becomes a struggle.
Expelled from paradise.	Humans will now have to make their own way in the world. God gave them the chance to have it all with him and they chose not to. In paradise, death and suffering were unknown. Not from now on. The world will be plagued by both until humanity repairs its relationship with God.

Textual work

The following is the kind of exam question on texts you may meet in your RMPS exam. NB: Remember, there are no prescribed sources at Intermediate 1

Read the following source then answer all parts of the question (a)–(e). The number of marks available for each part is indicated, use them to help you answer the question.

'Let us make them in our own image'

Gen 1:26

(a) What do Christians mean by the statement that humans are made 'in the image of God'?
(4 marks) KU

(b) What special role do Christians think humans have in the creation?
(4 marks) KU

(c) Explain what Christians mean by the term 'Original Sin'.
(8 marks) KU
(4 marks) AE

(d) What rights and responsibilities do Christians think humans are given as a result of being created in the image of God?
(6 marks) KU
(4 marks) AE

(e) Why is it important for Christians to accept that God created the Universe?
(3 marks) AE

(25 marks)

THE GOALS

Big Tam is in a football team. One day he goes to play a game against his team's biggest rivals. He gets changed, goes out to the pitch and stands on the sidelines refusing to play, even though he's meant to be playing. When asked why he's doing this he replies 'No point, the game will be over in 90 minutes anyway so I might as well just stand here until it's finished'.

Has Big Tam got a point or has he lost the plot?

Have you ever been in RMPS and heard a discussion go something like this?

> Pupil: 'Do we have to do this? What's the point of it all?'
> Teacher: 'What's the point of anything when you really think about it?'
> Pupil: 'Nothing. You're born you live, you die – and what for?'
> Teacher: 'Maybe the living it is what it's all about'
> Pupil: 'Yeah, Yeah … when does the bell go?'

What are your aims in life? Do you have any? What is the point of your existence? Is there any? Does whether you have any aims or not affect how you live? Does the fact that we will all die someday make everything seem pointless?

Sitting in class right now you must have some plans for the future. You must be aiming for something. What? Why? How important these goals are for you will affect most of the things you do. What if you have no goals? What kind of life might you lead? A different one? Are your goals realistic? What will you have to do to achieve them? Can you do it on your own?

Christians believe that there is a point to life. They believe it has meaning and purpose. We're not just stumbling around in the dark – we're heading somewhere. Our life is for something. And what about the end of life? This is something we all have in common. We will all die one day. Is that it? If planet earth has been around for millions of years and each human gets to live, on average, for about 70 years then our lives are truly a blink in the great scheme of things. Might anything happen to us after death? Should we plan for that to happen or not? Is a life after death something to look forward to or be afraid of? And what if there's nothing? Is that scary or not? Would that make any difference to how you live your life now?

Christians believe that death doesn't have to be the end – though there are different views about what happens. But Christians also believe that there is a point to living in the here and now. Some people have criticised Christians for having a 'death wish' – in other words, being so focused on the afterlife that they don't pay much attention to this one. Christians would disagree strongly.

Getting into it

◆ What are your goals in life?

◆ Do you think life has a point?

◆ What do you believe happens after death?

◆ What kind of life should you live?

◆ How can you get the most out of life?

◆ How much of your life should be about you and how much should it be about others?

◆ Does it make any sense to stand on the sidelines of life and just watch until it's all over?

◆ What are you aiming for in your life?

Loving God and Your Neighbour

Make your own good samaritan story

Fill in the blanks to make your very own story! (Don't offend anyone and try not to get too personal!)

Once upon a time [*some guy of your choice – famous or ordinary, you choose*] was walking [*somewhere dangerous where he was quite likely to get duffed up*]. As he walked he was attacked by [*a group of people who might well do such a thing round your way*]. They left him for dead. It just so happened that [*someone who is a person of some authority in your community/world*] walked past. S/he had a look and walked on by on the other side saying [*what might such a person say?*]. The man was horrified because he had thought that [*first person*] really would have helped him. Then [*someone else who is a fine upstanding member of your community/world*] appeared – but s/he walked on by too saying [*well, you're getting the hang of it now aren't you?*]. Finally, [*someone that the guy lying dying would be totally unlikely to expect any help from – in fact, he'll think this one won't help him but finish him off instead – maybe it's the victim's worst enemy*] appears. S/he kneels and helps the injured man, taking him to the nearest hospital. S/he writes a blank cheque and gives it to a nurse. 'Get him whatever he needs'. And then leaves.

Compare this story with Luke 10: 25–37

Time Out (23)

Do you know of any examples of someone being a 'good Samaritan' recently?

Loving others

Christians believe that possibly the most powerful human emotion is love. They don't just mean the slobbery kind, but something far more powerful. Christians believe in a kind of love called agape. This is practical love which is put into action. It is *unconditional* because it doesn't depend on the person loving you back – nor does it depend on how they look or how wealthy they are for example. Agape also means that you should even love those who are unlovable – for whatever reason – for example showing love towards a murderer or terrorist (but don't forget the idea of repentance from earlier!).

A Quaker view

Some central beliefs hold us together as a religious community:

◆ The light of God is in everyone.

◆ Each person can have a direct, personal relationship with God – there is no need for a priest or a minister as a mediator.

◆ Our relationship with God is nurtured by worship based on silent waiting.

◆ The nature of God is love.

These beliefs lead us to strive for:

◆ The equality of all human beings.

◆ Simplicity in our worship and in our way of life.

◆ Peace.

◆ Social justice.

◆ The right to freedom of conscience.

◆ A sense of shared responsibility for the life of our communities and the integrity of creation.

Source: http://website.lineone.net/~wirralchesterquakers/beliefs.htm

Talking Point (21)

Why is it difficult to show love to everyone?

Love isn't always easy, but is always right. Nowadays, people talk about tough love – that's a pretty good explanation for agape. Christian love is sometimes hard to do, but it's always right to do.

Jesus told the story of the Good Samaritan after telling some slippery expert in Jewish religious law that the most important commandment was to 'Love God and your neighbour'. This was an easy question to answer because Jesus just quoted from the Jewish scriptures in Deuteronomy 6: 5. But the legal eagle was trying to get Jesus to say something which would get him into trouble – so he asked, 'Who is my neighbour?'. Jesus told the story of the Good Samaritan and let the wise guy work it out for himself. The truth was that the Jews and Samaritans were bitter enemies – so who would have expected a Samaritan to help a Jew in need – especially one who had just been ignored by two of his own people? But the Samaritan did – putting the rest to shame. That's how much we should love others according to Jesus. We love them according to their need, no matter who they are or what they have done.

Roman Catholic view

All our thoughts and actions must be motivated by the message of love, which Jesus proclaims. Like the Samaritan our love must be spontaneous and generous, completely unhindered by customs or excuses, which might shield us from the demands of Christian love.

Source: Father Paul Townsend at http://www.sacred-heart.org.uk/newsletter-28.html

Talking Point (22)

What examples are there of enemies in today's world?

Christians see loving others as one of the main goals in life. It's a skill we all have to develop, but which, of course, we'd all benefit from. The Christian Bible teaches that you 'reap what you sow'. If you show love to others then you'll get that back in return.

How much love?

Is there a limit to how much you can love other people? Should you give it all away or keep some back? Should you only give what you can 'spare'? Christians believe that you should give as much as you can. Some people will be more able to help others and some will find it easier than others to show love. Jesus told the story of the widow's mite as an example of the value of giving what you can (See Luke 21: 1–4). People donating money at the Temple sometimes made a big song and dance about it – showing how wealthy they were by how much they were able to give away. They hoped that others would

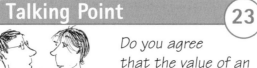

Talking Point (23)

Do you agree that the value of an action comes from the intention behind it?

Time Out (24)

Who are the unlovable in society today?

be impressed (they probably were). Their money probably did very good work. But Jesus told a parable about a poor widow who gave her last few pennies. He said that this was worth so much because it was everything she could give. So how much love should a Christian give to others? As much as it is possible to give – to everyone who needs it. If you give whatever you can then that's worth a lot.

Loving the unlovable

This is one Christian teaching which gets people a bit worked up. Surely some people don't deserve to be loved? Perhaps they have done something unbelievably awful or are thoroughly unlikable characters. What did Jesus say?

'Truly I tell you, you must love your enemies and pray for those who persecute you.'

'Aye right!' is probably your reaction to that. Was this just one of Jesus' big ideas – OK in theory but don't ask me to put it into practice? No. According to Christians, Jesus did show love to the unlovable. His life is full of examples of healing people who were thought of as unclean, forgiving people who had done unforgivable things and helping those who would have been thought of as the enemy – like Roman Soldiers themselves. He made friends with tax collectors, (collaborators with the occupying forces), prostitutes, outcasts, lepers – in fact Jesus got friendly with just about every kind of social misfit around. So much so that he shocked the powerful people in his day. Jesus showed by his actions that love is the right thing to do whether you like it or not, and no matter what other people think about it. Jesus knew that people would be shocked by a Samaritan helping a Jew – but the shock was the point. It's easy to love those you like, much harder to love those who you're 'not supposed' to love. Christian belief is quite simple: You should follow the teachings of Jesus, but also copy his actions.

Jesus told Christians to 'love one another as I have loved you'. That means without prejudice, without question and without limit. So, that's how Christians are supposed to live. He also befriended outcasts and made them feel like valuable people – so Christians should do that too.

What can love do?

The widow's few coins didn't break the bank – but were they worthless? There is a saying: 'There is no greater fool than he who does nothing because he can only do a little'. Showing love to others might be donating millions to the poor, 5p to a good cause, or it might just be a helpful word to your mates. Either way, the outcome's the same. Love does people good. Christians believe that one of the most important tasks in life is the creation of the Kingdom of God. This means creating the kind

of world God would like right here, right now. You don't have to wait 'til you die to get to heaven – you can experience it now on earth. The Kingdom of God is based on fairness, justice, equality and peace – all of which can come through showing love to others. It probably won't happen overnight though, but that's OK, these things take time. Christians believe that creating the Kingdom of God has to start somewhere – why not with you?

A Baptist view

As a fellowship our primary concern is to carry out the work of the Kingdom of God on earth. In doing this we want to encourage each member to become a true disciple of Jesus Christ, living his or her life under the guidance and power of the Holy Spirit. This Church will be a place in which the gifts of the Spirit are recognised and exercised. In all these things we will be governed by love, for one another, and for others.

Partick Baptist Church's Mission Statement at http://peelcom.com/partickchurches/baptist/

Talking Point (24)

What one thing could you do today to make the world a better place?

Have a look at
http://www.holyjoes.com/100ways.htm
for 100 ways.

Small beginnings are still beginnings. Jesus taught that the Kingdom of God is like a mustard seed (See Luke 13: 18–19). It starts tiny and grows into a fine plant. Creating a world of justice starts small – the love equivalent of a widow's mite (or a wee mustard seed) but it will grow. Christians believe that 'love conquers all' and that the correct response to everything is a loving response. This is creative and affirming whereas anything else is destructive and negative. Christians believe that love builds things – perhaps a new world for all.

Love for God and love for mankind

Remember that The Fall was all about the relationship between man and God going sour. How can that be built up again? Christians believe that the only way is through love in action. Loving your fellow humanity was what Jesus taught and showed by example – but he also said that loving God was just as important.

Time Out (26)

How could people show that they loved God?

In fact, Jesus made one dependent on the other. He taught that if you loved God then you would also love mankind. If you showed this love for God in your everyday actions then you couldn't help but show love to people too. Jesus told his disciples that any time they had seen anyone in need and ignored it, it was no different to seeing Jesus himself in need and ignoring that. (See Textual Sources section on pages 93–4.) It took the disciples a bit to work out the link, but they got the point eventually. So it's a simple equation really.

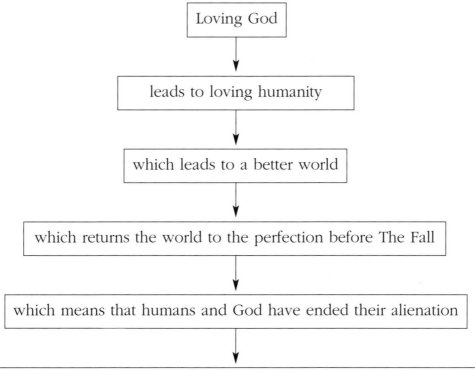

Loving God

↓

leads to loving humanity

↓

which leads to a better world

↓

which returns the world to the perfection before The Fall

↓

which means that humans and God have ended their alienation

↓

which means they have restored their relationship with God back to what it was intended to be in the first place.

Restoring the relationship between mankind and God is what being a Christian is all about. Showing love to others to make the world a better place isn't a bad goal to have in life. So one of the major goals in life is to establish God's kingdom on earth. You do this by getting the relationship with God right and you do that by loving God and your neighbour. Simple really.

'How can you love God, whom you do not see, if you do not love your neighbour whom you see, whom you touch, with whom you live?'

— *Mother Teresa.*

Activities

Knowledge, Understanding & Evaluation

1 In your own words, tell the story of the Good Samaritan as found in Luke 10: 25–37.

2 Explain two of the messages in the story.

3 What question was the story designed to answer?

4 Why was a Samaritan chosen as the hero?

5 Who would be a suitable hero in today's world?

6 When is love unconditional?

7 What is agape?

8 Who would you find it most difficult to show love to?

9 What evidence is there that the Quakers think putting love into action is important?

10 According to the Roman Catholic view on page 59, what two things should love not be hindered by?

11 Give an example from your own experience of each of these.

12 What could be the rewards of love?

13 How much love should a Christian give away?

14 How does the story of the widow's mite illustrate the value of giving what you can?

15 Why should Christian love lead to action?

16 In what way did the lifestyle of Jesus set an example for Christians about who they should care for?

17 Who might be shocked by the actions of Jesus if he returned today?

18 In what ways can love do people good?

19 What do Christians understand by the Kingdom of God?

20 What does Partick Baptist Church think about the Kingdom of God?

21 Christians think that love is the best response to everything. What do they mean? What do you think?

22 How does loving God lead to loving others?

23 Can love put right the alienation between man and God? How?

Practical Activities

1 Make up your own version of the Good Samaritan story. Set it in a modern context. Perhaps you could perform it at an assembly – or for your local primary schools to help them with their RME.

2 Prepare a short report on the work of the Samaritans. How did they begin? What do they do? And in what way is their work based on the parable? (See *www.samaritans.org.uk*)

3 Find out about the work of a Christian organisation in your area which loves the unlovable. Design a poster to advertise the work of this organisation and possibly raise money for its work. (If there's nothing in your area, find out about the work of the Bethany Christian Trust at ***www.bethanychristiantrust.com***. In what way does this organisation work with the "unlovable"?

4 Produce a piece of artwork entitled simply 'The unlovable'.

5 Prepare a display board for your classroom. In the centre write 'What could I do to make the world a more loving place?'. Each person in your class should write a statement beginning with 'I could . . .'.

Unit Assessment Question

I1 In the story of the Good Samaritan, what did the Samaritan do?   (4KU)

I2 In the story of the Good Samaritan, why would the ending have been a surprise for those listening to Jesus telling the story?   (2KU, 4AE)

Higher
What can a Christian learn from the story of the Good Samaritan?   (6)

Sample Exam Question

I1 Give an example of one way in which Jesus showed love to the 'unlovable'.   (3KU)

I2 According to Christians, how can love help heal the relationship between humans and God?   (6AE)

Higher
Explain how the life of Jesus was an example of how Christians should put love into action.   (4 KU, 4 AE)

Homework

List as many benefits as you can of living a more loving life. Be prepared to justify anything in your list in class.

Personal Reflection

What would being more loving of others do for your life?

Worship

> **Thousands of Teenagers Take Part in Mobile Phone Church Service**
>
> Thousands of teenagers are estimated to have followed the first ever mobile phone church service via SMS messages on their mobile phones.
>
> Some 2,500 teenagers watched the German service which flashed up Bible texts, the sermon, intercessions and blessings from the actual church service.
>
> The pews in the Evangelical Church in Hanover were empty as the congregation followed the sermon from home.
>
> Another 800 watched the service online via a webcam set up in the church.
>
> And virtual devotees even sent in requests for intercessions before the service which were then read out in church.
>
> The church says more SMS services are planned because the first interactive service was so successful in attracting young people.

Source: http://www.ananova.com/news/story/sm_282683.html?menu=news.technology

Talking Point 25

Why are teenagers so attached to their mobiles?

How often do you use your mobile? Who do you contact? How? How many text messages a day? How much do you spend on it? Do you ever find yourself texting someone or phoning them just after you've spent the whole day with them? People like to talk. People like to communicate.

Talking to God

Imagine your friends didn't phone or text you for a while. How long would it take before you thought they had fallen out with you? Christians think it is important to keep up their communication with God. When relationships break down, one of the common reasons given is that there

has been a breakdown in communication. After The Fall, and the alienation between God and mankind – that's exactly what happened. So, for Christians, re-establishing the lines of communication with God is very important. Maybe every so often Christians need to call up God and ask, 'How are you?' There are many ways in which Christians can communicate with God.

Public prayer

Private prayer

Charismatic prayer

School prayer

Private prayer

Time Out (27)

Have you ever prayed? When? Why? Was there any response. Discuss sensitively in class.

Prayer is talking to God, but it takes many forms.

More or less all Christians carry out private prayer. In this they might ask for God's help in something or they might ask for advice. They might ask for something for someone else. Asking for things is called supplication. Christians don't expect to get everything, but take things to God and let him decide. Private prayer can be spoken or not. Some people just like to sit and think things through. After all, God knows what you want and can hear you even without speaking. Private prayer might even be a form of meditation. This just means concentrating fully on something and focusing on that alone. It might be a worry or a Bible teaching or something which is on your mind. Meditation like this can help you understand something more clearly or, some Christians believe, still your mind so that the voice of God can answer you. During prayer, some Christians think that it is important to sit or kneel or stand. There are no hard and fast rules about that – just what you feel is best.

Christians believe their prayers are answered, though again there are different views about how this is done. Some have heard God speaking – literally. Others get what they have asked for – sometimes in a roundabout way, sometimes directly. Some say that they just get a clear idea of what to do next – maybe this is the way God works.

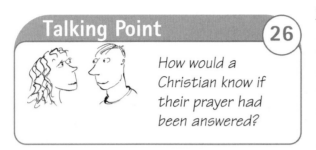

Talking Point 26

How would a Christian know if their prayer had been answered?

Most Christians believe that the individual can communicate directly with God. The role of priests or ministers as go-between varies throughout Christianity. In some denominations, like Roman Catholicism and Orthodoxy, the Priests have a central role as middlemen between man and God. Groups like the Brethren (Gospel Halls) tend to cut out the middlemen.

Public prayer

This can be anything from prayer rings – where groups agree to pray about the same things at the same time, not necessarily together – to large church services. Most Christians think it is important to pray together. Sometimes this is just listening to a priest or minister pray for you. Sometimes it is a set prayer like the Lord's Prayer. Sometimes it is responses to particular statements. Sometimes these prayers are well-known or prepared in advance – other times they just happen spontaneously. Prayers can be very formal or use everyday informal language. Christians believe that praying with others doesn't make God listen more, but it is a way of sharing common hopes and fears and communicating not only with God, but with each other. So praying, like love, has a God/person dimension as well as a person/person dimension.

Time Out 28

Should Christian worship be serious and somber or happy clappy? Discuss views in your class.

Some Christians believe in a form of prayer called speaking in tongues. They believe that this is a heavenly language and is a gift of the Holy Spirit. One person is given the gift of tongues and will speak in a way that can sound very strange. Another person will be given the gift of translating this – and they will tell what the tongues-speaker has been saying. Believers in this say that what they say has come direct from God. Speaking in tongues is often accompanied by lively, ecstatic worship.

Quakers, on the other hand have a very different approach to prayer and worship. In a Quaker service there is no singing or priests or formal prayers. Each member, known as a 'friend' sits in silence and waits for God to speak.

Individuals will speak when they feel they should and Quakers believe that this is also a way in which the Holy Spirit speaks to people.

In the Roman Catholic Church, prayers are often formal and responsive. The priest will usually lead the service with the congregation responding according to a printed order of service. Alternatively, in the Church of Scotland, there are fewer responsive prayers – prayers are generally led by the Minister or by a member of the congregation.

Talking Point 27

Is such variety in Christian approaches to prayer a good thing? Shouldn't Christians all do the same?

But here's the thing: In all versions of Christianity there is a great deal of variation. Prayer can be formal or informal, quietly reflective or wild and ecstatic. There are common elements to prayer throughout the faith, but some Churches are working on new ways to do things and others mix the new with the old – whatever the denomination. All have in common the idea of speaking and listening to God – keeping the lines of communication open.

Worship and spirituality – the sixth sense?

As well as prayer there are many ways Christians worship. Worship is a joyful experience designed to show love for God. It aims also to help believers support each other in their faith. It's not always easy being a Christian and worship helps some Christians re-charge their batteries so they can go out into the world and live a Christian life. Worship involves the spiritual dimension to life, but it can involve all the senses. It can be noisy or quiet, solemn or boisterous, dramatic or plain. As well as sights, sounds, tastes, smells and feelings – a human's five senses – worship appeals to a person's spiritual side too, perhaps developing and strengthening that spiritual link with God.

There are many common elements to worship even though these are put together in many different ways in different Christian traditions. What's common to them all?

◆ Praying and communicating with God.

◆ Thanking God and asking for his help – sometimes through singing hymns, choruses or chants.

◆ Listening to God – perhaps through a spiritual means or by listening to the word of God in Bible readings and study.

◆ Responding to God – through personal reflection or statements of commitment or giving.

◆ Supporting others in the Christian community and in the world – through preparation for action and mutual kindness.

Salvation Army worship

The Salvation Army style of worship has a certain degree of structure, particularly at meetings held on a Sunday, but largely encourages freedom of expression and regular participation by the congregation. This participation can be either individual (by praying, giving personal testimony, reading from the Bible or presenting a musical contribution) or communal (by united singing of hymns or united readings from the Bible). Within the service itself, specific music groups will often present a worship contribution. Sunday meetings always include a sermon, given to highlight the particular aspect of the Christian message. Sunday morning meetings also generally include a similar message (but simpler, and often light-hearted) for the children in the congregation.

Source: http://homepages.tesco.net/~irene.mcintosh1/portarmy/meetings.htm

For other forms of traditional worship see:
www.ocf.org/OrthodoxPage/liturgy/liturgy.html for an example of a traditional forma liturgy followed by the Orthodox Church and ***www.christusrex.org/www1/CDHN/mass.html*** for one followed by the Roman Catholic Church.

Time Out (29)

From what you have learned about the person of Jesus so far, what do you think he would think of a Christian group meeting for worship in a pub?

Alternative forms of worship

Nowadays, Christian worship is as wide and varied as are Christians themselves. Perhaps the only experience you've had of 'Christian worship' is school assemblies or weddings and funerals. There are many new forms of worship being devised by Christian groups including the Iona Community, a group called 'The Late Late Service' based in Glasgow, and a group called Holy Joe's (!) which meets in a London pub (see ***www.holyjoes.com/sacredspace.htm***).

For other forms of alternative worship, see ***www.alt-worship.org/altg.html***

Worship as a goal in life

Maybe not your first thought in answer to the question of what should I be doing with my life, but Christians think that worship is a good goal to have. Worship helps Christians to grow in their understanding of God and to develop their love for God. Worship helps to bring humanity and God back together again to re-establish the relationship by getting both communicating. By now you know why Christians think this matters. It also helps to glue fellow Christians together – this is part of what's meant by the Christian Community. Getting closer to God and your fellow mankind is therefore a goal for Christians.

Activities

Knowledge, Understanding & Evaluation

1 Why do you think the SMS Church service was a success?

2 Why do Christians think it is important to keep up the communication with God?

3 Describe three forms of Christian prayer.

4 Do you think Christians should pray out loud? Explain your answer.

5 In what way can prayer have a person/person dimension?

6 What is meant by speaking in tongues?

7 Explain one difference between prayer in a Roman Catholic Church and prayer in a Church of Scotland.

8 How do Quakers pray and worship?

9 What, in your opinion, are the advantages and disadvantages of Quaker worship?

10 How could worship 're-charge a Christian's batteries'?

11 Do you think people have a spiritual side?

12 State two common elements in most forms of Christian worship.

13 Describe worship in the Salvation Army.

14 Describe worship in the Orthodox Church.

15 Why can worship be thought of as a goal for Christians?

Practical Activities

1 Meditation in Christianity is often used as a form of prayer. In Roman Catholicism, Rosary Beads are often used as an aid to prayer. Find out how this is done and what this means. Design an information leaflet about the use of Rosary Beads.

2 At times of disasters and problems, Christians (and often people who aren't) get together and pray. What kinds of things might they say or ask for? Devise a Christian prayer in response to something in the world which has happened recently which people might feel the need to pray for. Make this prayer something which could be said by all – or at least listened to without offence.

3 In many schools in Scotland there are religious assemblies as forms of worship. Have a class debate about whether this is right or not – presenting both sides of the argument. You could invite people in from outside school to present both cases or research and write them yourselves. Can school assembly really be called worship?

4 Devise a form of Christian worship which would appeal to people of your age. It can be sombre or party-like, it's up to you. Try to include the elements in the bullet points on pages 69–70.

Unit Assessment Question

I1 State one element in Christian worship. (1KU)

I2 Which part of worship might a Christian say is the most important? Give reasons for your answer. (1KU, 4AE)

Higher
What are the purposes of worship for Christians? (8)

Sample Exam Question

I1 'Public prayer is more important than private prayer'. Would a Christian agree? Give one reason for your answer. (4AE)

I2 Why is worship important to Christians? (4AE)

Higher
Describe two forms of Christian prayer. (4 KU)

Homework

Find a website of alternative approaches to Christian worship. Write a brief report on the site.

Personal Reflection

Could (does) prayer contribute anything to your life?

Easter and the Resurrection

Robbie and Don are at a trendy nightclub in Inverness. They're not exactly attracting the female dancers so Robbie reaches into his pocket and produces a little foil-wrapped chocolate egg.

ROBBIE: Here Don, you want a cream egg?

DON: Is it, you know, OK?

ROBBIE: Aye, course it is, it's just a cream egg ya numpty.

DON: Aw, I see, just a cream egg is it?

ROBBIE: It's Easter tomorrow after all, in't it?

DON: So it is.

ROBBIE: What aboot Jesus then?

DON: Jesus who? Is he the DJ the night?

ROBBIE: Naw, Jesus, you know the wan in that Mel Gibson film?

DON: The Rab Roy wan?

ROBBIE: Naw, Jesus, J e s u s – of Nazareth. God's wee boy. The wan that got crucifixed. D'ye no think he was sumthin' else?

DON: Aye, I suppose he was a great guy. Some really good ideas there I think. Pity people canny put them intae action.

ROBBIE: Aye, he did have some good ideas, but what aboot efterwards?

DON: Efterwards whit?

ROBBIE: You know, comin back tae life and all that.

DON: Oh aye, that regression.

ROBBIE: Resurrection ya eejit.

DON: Naw, I'm no sure aboot that. I think that wis just made up tae make the story a wee bit more interesting. There's nae proof.

ROBBIE: Whit aboot his followers seein him alive efter he'd been deid. That's pretty good proof is it no?

DON: Naw people were just upset. They just wanted him tae come back, so they hallucinated. Just like some of the people here the night I think.

ROBBIE: Right, so these disciples of his. When he wis killed they ran away and hid. They were scared silly. They didn't even want tae admit they knew him.

DON: So?

ROBBIE: So, three days later they come oot of hiding. They tell everybody they've seen him and he's back fae the dead and gone tae heaven tae his Da. Nae fear, nae worries. Whit's changed?

DON: Aye, I suppose that is a bit weird.

ROBBIE: Weird? Three days before they'd been the biggest scaredy cats in the universe and now they're the bravest.

DON: Or the dumbest.

ROBBIE: Naw, they saw him right enough.

DON: So, even if they did – so what? Does it make his teaching any better?

ROBBIE: Maybe no, but here's the thing. If he can beat death, does that mean we can as well?

DON: Now there's an idea. Mind you that's probably easier than you chattin up that lassie over there.

ROBBIE: Don, watch and learn. Hi Doll, fancy a bit of cream egg ...?

The problem of the Resurrection

> ## Talking Point (28)
>
> What views are there in your class about the Resurrection of Jesus?

Did the Resurrection happen? That could be a book in itself – anyway you should have thought that one through in RMPS by now! What's important here is what Christians believe. After being crucified, Christians believe that Jesus rose from

death on the third day and soon afterwards ascended into heaven to be with his father, God. All of this happened just the way he had predicted it would. This was a supernatural event, central to Christian belief. For many people – even those who accept the message of Jesus in his teachings – this part is hard to take. Death is death. How can you cheat it? But Christians believe that Jesus did and that this gives added power to the things he taught – because if he was right about coming back from the dead then he must have been right about everything else. Again, believing in the Resurrection is an act of Christian faith – no proof needed.

Christian views

> The Belfast Chinese Christian Church says this about Jesus. It believes in:
>
> The full deity of the Lord Jesus Christ, the Incarnate Son of God; His virgin birth and His real and sinless humanity; His death on the cross, His bodily resurrection and His present reign in heaven.
>
> *Source: http://www.tay.org/bccc/beliefs.htm*

From the Roman Catholic Church:

After Jesus died on the cross, his body was laid in a tomb and his soul descended to the dead, just like all souls before him. But he, however, went there as a Saviour, to release the just souls who had waited to be set free by him, so that they could join him in Heaven. His body was buried in a tomb and remained there for nearly three days . Then, on the third day, by his power as God, he rose from the dead to the new and eternal life of the Resurrection. This is called 'the Resurrection of Jesus from the Dead'.

Source: http://www.catholic.org.uk/library/catechism/whoroseagain.shtml

Time Out 30

Why do people today seem to want proof of everything?

God made flesh

All through the Jewish scriptures there are prophecies about a Messiah who will come from God and save God's people. This will be painful and hard to do, and he will be rejected by people, just like they had rejected God's attempts to restore their relationship with him again and again. Christians believe that Jesus was that Messiah. They believe that Jesus was God's only son. God sent his son to live among us, to teach and to show by example how we should live our lives. Christians believe that in every sense Jesus was a complete human and in every sense he was completely God. Jesus was the Incarnation of God – quite literally, God made flesh. So, on the cross, God died too.

Talking Point 29

What good would it do for God to become human?

This means that God could experience directly what it was like to go through every human experience and emotion – to understand his creation through becoming it. It also means that in the person of Jesus, God and mankind became as one – showing what was possible. Jesus was raised from death – showing that when a human accepts God completely – death no longer has any power over you.

Time Out 31

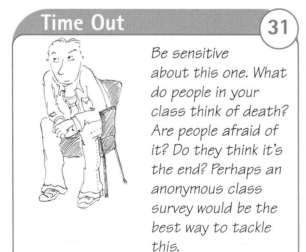

Be sensitive about this one. What do people in your class think of death? Are people afraid of it? Do they think it's the end? Perhaps an anonymous class survey would be the best way to tackle this.

Keeping promises, safeguarding freedom

Remember that God wanted to put right his and mankind's fall-out. Christians believe that the Resurrection is final proof that God keeps his promises. God shows how much he loves his creation by sending his son and putting him through a fairly miserable experience to get the message through to people. Christians believe that Jesus is God's final attempt to get people back. If they don't respond to this then what else could he do? But why didn't he just appear

– well, more God-like? This again is one of God's ways of safeguarding human freedom and choice. If God had just appeared as God in a blaze of supernatural glory, then people would be forced to believe in him. They'd have no choice. So, to make sure they did have a choice, God chose to come among humans in Jesus, in the way that he did. So, you can accept the life, death and resurrection of Jesus if you want – or not.

Yes, and not just to nice people

Jesus' death and resurrection turned Adam's choice around. Remember Adam had rejected God's will. Jesus accepted it. In the garden of Gethsemane, Jesus prayed

that God would take away the suffering and pain he was about to go through. His human self was just plain scared. But he finished this prayer with 'Not my will, but yours'. Christians believe this put right Adam's mistake. A human had now agreed to the relationship between God and man. Jesus was now the new Adam.

Roman Catholic view

Jesus' cry on the Cross, dear Brothers and Sisters, is not the cry of anguish of a man without hope, but the prayer of the Son who offers his life to the Father in love, for the salvation of all. At the very moment when he identifies with our sin, 'abandoned' by the Father, he 'abandons' himself into the hands of the Father. His eyes remain fixed on the Father. Precisely because of the knowledge and experience of the Father which he alone has, even at this moment of darkness he sees clearly the gravity of sin and suffers because of it. He alone, who sees the Father and rejoices fully in him, can understand completely what it means to resist the Father's love by sin. More than an experience of physical pain, his Passion is an agonizing suffering of the soul.

Apostolic letter Novo millennio ineunte of his holiness Pope John Paul II (2000)

Talking Point (30)

Why might Jesus have been a bit worried about what was going to happen to him if he knew how it would all end anyway?

But it wasn't enough just to say it, he had to go through with it. People wonder why Jesus let this happen to himself. He had to – he couldn't agree to God's plan and then cheat at the last minute. That's what Adam did. So, by accepting the decisions of God and by going through with the death, Jesus restored the relationship between man and God broken at The Fall. The benefits of the Resurrection are there for everyone. In return, God kept his promise of restoring Jesus, to life. With Adam, death found a way in, with Jesus, death was put well and truly in its place. The Resurrection was final proof of God's love. Final proof that he would keep his promises. Final proof that getting it right with God was a pretty good idea.

Free Church of Scotland view

The doctrine of the Resurrection of the Lord Jesus Christ from the dead teaches us many things. He obtained the power and authority to quicken dead sinners because, by His sufferings unto death, He laid a foundation in justice by which He obtained the authority to forgive sins (Isaiah 53: 11; Matthew 9: 6). By Christ's resurrection from the dead, God is declaring that salvation has been accomplished. He suffered upon the cross of Calvary, and freely, willingly, and lovingly laid down His life as a substitutionary sacrifice in the place of His people so that the wrath of God which was due to them for their sins might be taken away.

Source: http://home.rednet.co.uk/homepages/fpchurch/EbBI/fpm/1998/July/article2.htm

Washing away the stain

When you looked at The Fall, the idea of sin was described as a stain you couldn't wash away. Christians believe that the death of Jesus washed the sin away. His blood as a sacrifice wiped clean mankind's dim record of sin. Of course, people could still sin, but Jesus had showed how it was possible not to, as Christians believe that he lived and died without sin. But he also showed that sin didn't need to have a hold on you. You could beat it. You could send it down the plug-hole by accepting the meaning and consequences of the Resurrection:

◆ Jesus' resurrection was proof that he was who he said he was – what more proof do you need than that he overcame death?

◆ So the Resurrection was proof of the power of God.

◆ The Resurrection gives everyone a great big chance to say yes to God once and for all.

◆ Death's power is shown to be in God's hands.

◆ God's great love for his creation is shown in the great sacrifice he makes of his only son.

◆ Everyone can share in the benefits of the Resurrection by accepting Jesus.

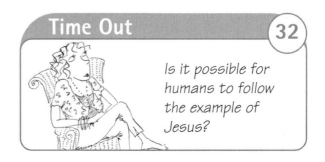

Time Out   32

Is it possible for humans to follow the example of Jesus?

Easter: Eggs and crosses

The Christian festival of Easter celebrates the Resurrection. Much of what passes for Christian celebration is an odd mixture of Christian ideas and pre-Christian ideas. For example, the pagan goddess of spring was called Eostre. Eggs were symbols of the Norse goddess Ostara. In the Mediterranean area, the pre-Christian god Attis was believed to have died and risen three days later. What's going on?

Christians believe that one of the most powerful messages of the Resurrection is the idea of new life. Being born again, being freed from the power of death are all common themes. So too are celebrations of springtime. Christians celebrate the Resurrection at springtime because the meanings of both events are similar. Also, as Christianity spread it adopted local customs and ideas into its own way of thinking. Nothing odd here – all Christians did was replace things with Christian explanations which, of course, they think were better. For example, many Christians have dawn services to welcome the Son on Easter morning – just like pagans welcome the Sun at the same time. Christians would say that if some already existing idea helps to explain Christian beliefs then why not use it? So at Easter time, Christians roll eggs as symbols of the stone that was rolled away from Jesus's tomb; they use images of chicks as symbols of new life, just like Jesus stood for the chance of a new life. So Christian ideas are mixed with non-Christian ones, but the message is the same. Easter is the time of God's promise of new life. It's a time of hope based on the gift of Jesus and his Resurrection.

Talking Point 31

How (and why) do you celebrate Easter?

Orthodox Pascha celebration

Pascha, or Easter as it is known to you, is the most important festival in the Orthodox Church. The service is very dramatic and symbolises the sadness and despair of the death of Jesus compared with the joy and hope of his Resurrection.

A typical service would go something like this:

On Good Friday, the death of Jesus is remembered. The mood in church is very solemn and serious. People dress in black. There is a cloth carried round with an icon of Jesus on it. At midnight just before Easter Sunday the congregation will be in the church standing. The priests will be behind the altar screen and all is dark. People will hold candles but they are not lit yet. At midnight the bells ring out and the doors of the altar are thrown open. The priests appear dressed in white and bright colours. They shout, 'Christ is risen!' and everyone replies 'He is risen indeed!' They come round and light candles to symbolise Jesus as the light of the world. The Church is now bright and happy symbolising the joy of the Resurrection.

Orthodox Christian view

In these events the Orthodox Church re-enacts in a dramatic and very human way in order to move, instruct and guide her children. This is because these events, as well as everything else connected with Christ, are of basic existential and eternal significance for us Christians. They refer to the love of God who sent down His only Son to save the world from sin, death, corruption and eternal annihilation. For the plain truth is that Christ's presence in the world constitutes the highest, most perfect and final decision of God to share the human tragedy.

His Eminence Archbishop Gregorios of Thyateira and Great Britain – http://www.orthodox-christian-comment.co.uk/pascha-thyateirapascha-2003.htm

The Resurrection – made for sharing

The Resurrection wasn't just God showing-off. It was an example for all. Quite simply it means that if you accept Jesus you can share in the benefits of the Resurrection. That's got two sides. Firstly, you can benefit from the life and teachings of Jesus now because you know it was right – the Resurrection proves it. Secondly, you too can enjoy your very own Resurrection if you say yes to God just like Jesus did. Some Christians call this being 'born again'. They believe that it is a new beginning and a new kind of life, lived like Jesus' example, not like Adam's. If you're born again some of the usual things don't apply to you – like death. Now there are different Christian views about what resurrection actually means – is it physical or spiritual, because obviously everyone's body dies. Jesus' resurrected body gives us a clue. It was neither completely physical nor was it just spirit like some kind of ghost. Whatever resurrection means in practice for our own bodies and souls, Christians agree on this: If you accept Jesus, then death is not the end for you. We'll look at what that might mean in the next section.

Activities

Knowledge, Understanding, Evaluation

1 What does Robbie think is very good evidence that the Resurrection happened?

2 Why do some people find the Resurrection difficult to accept?

3 What is meant by a Messiah?

4 In what way do Christians think the Jewish scriptures are linked to the life of Jesus?

5 What does Incarnation mean?

6 In what ways is the Incarnation important for Christians?

7 How might it help you to believe that God became a human?

8 Why was God sending his son an act of love on God's part?

9 Why didn't God just appear as God?

10 What did Jesus' acceptance of God's will do to Adam's actions in The Fall?

11 According to the Roman Catholic view on page 78, what is the Passion of Jesus all about?

12 How did Jesus restore the mankind/God relationship?

13 According to the Free Church of Scotland's view on page 78, in what way was Jesus' death a sacrifice?

14 How did Jesus' death wash away sin?

15 State two consequences of the Resurrection.

16 Why do you think the Orthodox Church prefers the word Pascha to describe what you know as Easter?

17 Describe two things which happen during Orthodox Pascha celebrations.

18 How does symbolism help Christians in their understanding of the Resurrection?

19 What does it mean to be 'born again'?

20 In what way is the Resurrection centred on the idea of hope?

Practical Activities

1 Find out how Christian churches in your area celebrate Easter. What services take place, what symbols are used. Write an illustrated article for a teenage magazine about this.

2 In the Roman Catholic Church, the stations of the cross are used to illustrate the events of the death and resurrection of Jesus. Make your own artistic versions of these. (See

www.tcweb.co.uk/stationsofthecross/ for a brilliant exhibition of art on stations of the cross from West Glasgow New Church.)

3 A famous poem by Canon Henry Scott Holland aims to demonstrate the Christian belief that death is not the end. (See *www.liamdelahunty.com/victor/funeral%20poetry.txt.*) Using the idea of

the Resurrection of Jesus, write your own piece of poetry reflecting the Christian belief that Jesus has conquered death.

4 Draw up a table of symbols used at Easter. Identify those which are Christian and those which are not. Show clearly how Christian meanings have been attached to non-Christian symbols.

Unit Assessment Question

I1 State one way in which Easter celebrations remember the Resurrection of Jesus. (2KU)

I2 State one way in which the Resurrection of Jesus is important for a Christian. (2KU)

Higher
According to Christians, why did Jesus rise from the dead? (10)

Sample Exam Question

I1 What would a Christian mean by saying that Jesus' death 'washed away sin'? (4KU)

I2 'Without the Resurrection, the story of Jesus would have no meaning'. How might a Christian respond to this statement? (2KU, 4AE)

Higher
'For Christians, Jesus was the new Adam.' What would a Christian mean by saying this? (4 KU, 4 AE)

Homework

Design a piece of artwork entitled 'Resurrection'.

Personal Reflection

What or who do you make sacrifices for?

THE GOALS

Judgement, Heaven, Hell and Eternal Life

In the book *The Five People you Meet in Heaven*, Mitch Albom suggests an interesting idea. When you die you meet five people. Each of these people has played a part in your life – though you might not have known it. Their job is to gradually reveal to you what your life has been all about. Eddie, a maintenance man at a fairground, dies trying to save a child from a failed fairground ride. He learns what his life was for. But interestingly it's not exactly clear what happens to the five people he met once they've played their part in his story. Nor do we know what happens to Eddie once the meaning of his life has been revealed.

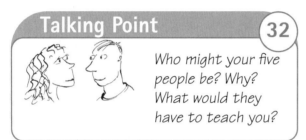

Talking Point (32)

Who might your five people be? Why? What would they have to teach you?

Jesus II

What's the sequel to the Jesus story? What happened to him after his Resurrection? What will happen to us?

Christian views about this show some variation, though again there are common elements throughout the faith – for example:

◆ Death is not the end.

◆ What happens afterwards is linked to the life you have lived.

◆ After death there are two options – with God or without.

◆ Christians believe that after death there will be a Resurrection for believers – physical, spiritual or both.

◆ Jesus' own death and Resurrection are the model for this.

Remember that Jesus was raised from death because he accepted the will of God. He put himself through pain and suffering because that's what God wanted from him. He had

Time Out (33)

Would an afterlife with God be better than one without?

his normal human doubts but in the end said yes to God. So God judged him a good guy.

Judgement

When you were younger your parents probably used Santa as a way to get you to behave well around Christmas time. 'Santa will be watching you' they might have said. You maybe even had an idea of Santa at the North Pole watching your every move on some TV screen. Some people might think of God that way – including some Christians probably – and who's to say they're wrong? Traditionally, Christians believe that God knows what they're up to. Nothing is hidden from him. God is Omniscient (all knowing). He pretty much knows what you're going to do before you do it anyway. Perhaps he writes it in a Big Book, or more likely a hand-held computer these days. Or perhaps it is just recorded in some other way – like the filing cabinet in *Bruce Almighty*. But what's he looking for? Earlier you looked at the idea of Salvation by works and by grace. Some people still think of God's judgement as a weighing up process like on a set of scales. Your bad deeds are on one side and your good on the other. If your bad deeds outweigh your good ones then you've had it. To an extent, Christians would not disagree with that though things are never that simple.

Christians do believe that you should live a good life. Your good works should outweigh your bad ones. But works are just what follow from your beliefs. No matter how good your works are, if your beliefs are wrong then a lifetime of good deeds might

Time Out (34)

If this turned out to be your last day on earth what would your good/bad scales look like?

not amount to much. In other words, after death you will be judged on whether you have chosen to accept God or not, because if you have, then good works will follow. No matter how good you are it's never going to be enough to make you perfect for the moment of judgement – but your beliefs can do the trick. If you have accepted the life, teachings and example of Jesus then you share in his yes to God. That's what makes your judgement go smoothly – not what you've done. Christians believe that it's simple cause and effect – you accept God, he accepts you. Your acceptance leads to living a good life and being judged favourably.

Elim Pentecostal view of judgement

The Future State

We believe in the resurrection of the dead and in the final judgement of the world, the eternal conscious bliss of the righteous and the eternal conscious punishment of the wicked.

Source: http://www.elimg.freeserve.co.uk/beliefs.html

When does judgement happen?

Again there are slightly different views on this. Some Christians think that you are judged straight after death. Others believe that you are raised up on a day called Judgement Day when everyone who has ever lived is judged at the same time. Some think it's a bit of both. After you die you have no experience of time so that you are raised on Judgement day like everyone else but it feels for you like a moment after your death. It doesn't matter whether you died five minutes or five thousand years before Judgement Day itself. On this day, Jesus teaches that people will be judged and separated like a shepherd separates sheep from goats (Matthew 25: 31). In fact he'll be there in person to do the judging – another good reason for taking his life and teachings seriously. How compassionate you have been in your life will be examined – so obviously what you have done is not unimportant – but remember that for most Christians these things are based on what you believe. Jesus will separate people into those who have been faithful to him (the righteous) and those who have not (the unrighteous). After this separation, the really spooky bit happens.

Roman Catholic view

1038 The resurrection of all the dead, 'of both the just and the unjust', will precede the Last Judgement. This will be 'the hour when all who are in the tombs will hear [the Son of man's] voice and come forth, those who have done good, to the resurrection of life, and those who have done evil, to the resurrection of judgement.' Then Christ will come 'in his glory, and all the angels with him ... Before him will be gathered all the nations, and he will separate them one from another as a shepherd separates the sheep from the goats, and he will place the sheep at his right hand, but the goats at the left ... and they will go away into eternal punishment, but the righteous into eternal life.'

Source: Catholic Catechism at http://www.vatican.va/archive/ENG0015/__P2P.HTM.

1016 By death the soul is separated from the body, but in the resurrection God will give incorruptible life to our body, transformed by reunion with our soul. Just as Christ is risen and lives for ever, so all of us will rise at the last day.

Source: http://www.vatican.va/archive/ENG0015/__P2J.HTM

Upstairs or downstairs?

Talking Point (33)

Some Christians do not believe in cremation or organ donation because the physical body must be whole for Judgement Day. What do you think of this?

Matthew 25: 41 doesn't mince its words:

'Then he will say to (the unrighteous) "Depart from me you who are cursed, into the eternal fire prepared for the devil and his angels"'. Ouch. From this one verse has come artwork throughout the ages – hellfire and brimstone sermons and Christians quite literally putting the fear of God into others. The traditional view of hell is a place of eternal torment. Unimaginable horrors. Where you'll wish you'd never been born. And what's more, it'll go on forever. Some Christians do accept this as the literal truth. You live your life, take your chances and then suffer the consequences.

Orthodox view of Hell

The Orthodox Church understands hell as a place of eternal torment for those who wilfully reject the grace of God. Our Lord once said, 'If your hand makes you sin, cut it off. It is better for you to enter into life maimed, than having two hands, to go to hell, into the fire that never shall be quenched – where their worm does not die, and the fire is not quenched' (Mark 9: 44–45). There is a day of judgement coming, and there is a place of punishment for those who have hardened their hearts against God. It does make a difference how we will live this life. Those who of their own free will reject the grace and mercy of God must forever bear the consequences of that choice.

Source: http://www.threeq.com/churches/orthodoxchurces.html

Quakers and the after-life

Friends do not consider a life after death as a reward for virtue, or as a compensation for the suffering in their lives on earth. Neither has the fear or threat of damnation been used to induce Friends to live better lives. The Quaker view of what happens beyond death is firmly rooted in the experience of this life.

Friends do not dogmatise about what happens after death. There are Friends who are convinced that there is an after-life, and those who are convinced that there is not. But all Friends feel that it is more important to get on with living this life, and seek to improve the conditions of humanity in this world, than to engage in speculations about the next.

Source: http://www.qnorvic.com/quaker/goatfwcc.html

Time Out 35

If hell is the worst thing you can imagine. What would your hell be?

Other Christians have a more symbolic understanding of it – thinking of hell as a place where God is absent – and that would be hell in itself. Also, rather than a place, some think of hell as a state of existence where the consequences of rejecting God stretch out for all eternity. But hang on. Some modern Christians are a little troubled by the idea of hell:

◆ If there is a hell then how can God be said to be a forgiving God – surely you should get another chance? Traditional Roman Catholic teaching thinks you can in Purgatory, see below.

Roman Catholic view of Purgatory

> 1030 All who die in God's grace and friendship, but still imperfectly purified, are indeed assured of their eternal salvation; but after death they undergo purification, so as to achieve the holiness necessary to enter the joy of heaven.

Source: http://www.vatican.va/archive/ENG0015/__P2N.HTM

Other reasons are:

◆ God is everywhere – how then can he be absent from hell?

◆ If the Devil is in charge of hell (as some traditional views have it) why is God letting him enjoy himself at other people's expense?

◆ Even if you were bad every moment of your average 70 years of human life – is *eternal* punishment really fair? Sounds a bit over the top.

◆ If God has given you free will, why does he punish you because you choose not to accept him?

These are difficult questions for Christians and many different ways of trying to cope with them have been tried. So what's the bottom line? One Christian explanation just links actions to reactions. If I drop something it falls. I can neither blame or praise the object for falling – it just did. Heaven and Hell are the same. Accepting God leads to Heaven, rejecting God leads to Hell. Simple cause and effect.

And what about Heaven? Harps? Angels? Fluffy clouds? Heaven too has suffered from traditional views throughout the ages. Eternally praising God? Again, some Christians take a literal view of Angels and Archangels and Ethereal diadems ... However, there are more symbolic understandings too. Heaven is being in the presence of God for all eternity. It is the logical consequence of accepting God. It might be spiritual or physical but none of that really matters. What does is that it is a complete restoration of your relationship with God. Back to the way it was for Adam before he famously slipped up. Heaven is a return to the ideal state of human/God relationships which existed in the beginning. It's the way

Talking Point (34)

Have you ever had any mental images of Heaven or Hell? (Do you now?) What were/are they?

God intended things to be and the best option for mankind. Heaven is when God and mankind are best friends again.

Do you have to die first?

For those Christians who do not see Heaven as a place but as a state of existence the answer is no. Obviously your physical body has limitations, but your soul or spirit doesn't. However, you can enjoy all the benefits of 'Heaven' right here and now. If Heaven means living in the presence of God then that can be started without any delay and no need to wait until you die. In fact, if it did, then you might wonder why Christians don't spend all their time wishing for death so that they can be with God. Christians believe that the Eternal life which has been promised by God is available right away by accepting Jesus. This is what Christians mean by the idea of being 'born again'. Instead of being born into a new physical life you are born into a new spiritual life. One in which you live in God and in a full relationship with him. You mirror the life lived by Jesus and so you get the same benefits.

Talking Point   35

What might be the benefits of being born again?

Eternal life

Accepting God through accepting Jesus is what Christians think brings eternal life. It frees humans from the limitations of being humans and gives them the promise that they are now part of God's Kingdom and ready to share in all the benefits which that brings. God chooses to engage in a relationship with humans for always – things return to the way they were meant to be.

Methodist teaching on eternal life

John Wesley taught the Four Alls:

◆ All need to be saved.

◆ All can be saved.

◆ All can know they are saved.

◆ All can be saved completely.

By 'saved' Wesley means, being saved from the present and future consequences of our human sinfulness inherited from Adam, by the atoning death of Christ upon the cross and the consequent sharing of a new and eternal life with God made possible by the Resurrection of Jesus Christ from the dead. All this may sound to some, an old-fashioned mouthful, but it simply means that the love of God, through faith in Jesus, can transform our lives for time and eternity.

So, for Christians, the ultimate goal in life is to enjoy being in the eternal presence of God. You get towards this by loving God and your fellow mankind. The reward is the best reward you can possibly get. This all sounds quite nice really – so how do you get it? More on this later.

Activities

Knowledge, Understanding, Evaluation

1 State three things Christians think the Jesus story tells us about death.

2 Why did Jesus put himself through pain and suffering?

3 What does the word Omniscient mean?

4 What are the implications for people of the idea of God's omniscience?

5 According to Christians, what kinds of things will you be judged on in the after life?

6 Are good works more important than right beliefs?

7 In what way is life on earth and the after life linked?

8 What's the difference between the righteous and the unrighteous?

9 What does the Elim Pentecostal Church think will happen to the wicked?

10 What do Christians believe will happen on Judgement day?

11 Why do you think the Roman Catholic Church does not agree with the cremation of the dead?

12 What does the Roman Catholic Church think will happen to body and soul on Judgement Day?

13 According to the Orthodox Church why is how you live your life important?

14 What do Quakers think about the after-life?

15 Is there *any* value in speculating about Heaven and Hell?

16 Why are some Christians unhappy with the idea of Hell?

17 What is Purgatory?

18 Describe a symbolic understanding of Heaven.

19 When can Eternal Life begin?

20 What do Christians mean when they talk about being 'born again'?

21 In what ways could Heaven be like the Garden of Eden?

22 In what way does a Christian think of Eternal Life as a goal?

Practical Activities

1 Write your own version of *The Five People you Meet in Heaven*. What would their stories be? What might your purpose in life be?

2 Imagine you are standing in front of God on Judgement Day. With reference to your beliefs and actions in

life – what might your conversation be like? Write the dialogue.

3 Make your own artistic representations of Heaven and/or Hell. These can be paintings/drawings or 3D sculptures.

4 If you were 'born again' as some Christians teach, what would your new life be like? (If you've already been 'born again' describe how this came about and what happened afterwards.)

Unit Assessment Question

I1 What do Christians believe will happen on the day of Judgement? (4KU)

I2 What might a Christian think is 'the ultimate goal in life'? (2KU)

Higher
How would a Christian justify the existence of Hell? (10)

Sample Exam Question

I1 'Doing good works cannot save you'. Would a Christian agree? Give reasons for your answer. (4AE)

I2 'Christians are saved by grace alone'. Outline two possible Christian responses to this statement. (4KU, 6AE)

Higher
How far do Christians believe that how you live your life has eternal consequences? (4 KU, 4 AE)

Homework

Write a poem, 'My idea of Hell' (please don't mention individual teachers).

Personal Reflection

If there is a Heaven and a Hell, what are the consequences of this for your life?

Textual Sources

Luke 10: 25–37

Jesus used parables to get points across. They create lasting visual images in your mind and so they're great teaching tools. People forget ideas, but they rarely forget a story. Jesus is asked to state what is the greatest teaching which he replies is to Love God and Your Neighbour. He explains who your neighbour is by telling a story. In Jesus' day it wasn't uncommon for people to have discussions like this in the street (is it any different today?). It was especially important for people to get to grips with what Jesus taught because of the claims that were being made about who he was. Some have tried to excuse the Priest and the Levite's actions by saying that they wouldn't want to become ritually unclean by touching a dead body. This is a pretty poor defence though because compassion always comes before ritual. The story's message is that you should help whoever needs help – regardless of who they are. Your neighbour is anyone to whom you can be neighbourly.

Luke 13: 18–24

Jesus suggests that starting off the kind of world God wants will be a small endeavour and maybe even a slow process but it will work and grow. The leaven in the bread stops it being flat and dull. It takes only a small bit to make the whole thing rise. Jesus' followers were relatively few. Today, Christians are around one third of the world's population. Looks as if the seed has grown.

Luke 21: 1–4

Jesus is making a contrast between showy giving and the more quiet kind. What's important is that the widow is left with nothing – she keeps nothing for herself. This is what Jesus expects from Christians – that they keep nothing back from themselves and also expect no showy reward for it. Their reward will not come from people being impressed by them but by God seeing what they have done.

> ### Matthew 25: 31–46
>
> Jesus reminds his followers that he will return again and judge them. He contrasts their fine words about helping others with the reality. He is suggesting that in every person you should 'see the person of Jesus'. If Christians looked at everyone as someone who is a reflection of Jesus then perhaps they'd treat everyone better. Jesus taught that he and God were the same. Christians have a duty to care for God's creation, including his creatures – including other humans. Christians should not help others to get something back, but because it is right in itself – though the consequences of not helping others aren't good. The reader is left in little doubt that those who do good will be rewarded and those who are wicked will be punished.

Textual work

The following is the kind of exam question you may meet in your RMPS exam. NB: Remember, there are no prescribed sources at Intermediate 1

Read the following source then answer all parts of the question 1 (a)–(f). The number of marks available for each part is indicated, use them to help you answer the question.

Luke 21: 1–4

(a) Whose behaviour is Jesus contrasting in this passage?
(4 marks) KU

(b) What do Christians believe are the outcomes of positive and negative actions in life?
(4 marks) KU

(c) Explain two Christian views on the importance of believing that Hell exists.
(6 marks) KU
(4 marks) AE

(d) 'All Christians should aim to get to Heaven.' How far would Christians support this statement? You should refer to two Christian traditions in your answer.
(4 marks) KU
(4 marks) AE

(e) Should a Christian be 'born again'?
(3 marks) AE

(f) 'Like the widow, God will reward Christians for their good actions.' To what extent is this true?
(2 marks) KU
(4 marks) AE

(31 marks)

People spend thousands of pounds a year on their holidays. Sometimes they're in debt for the rest of the year to get two weeks 'away from it all'. But ... how many people about 10 days into their holiday, say things like 'I've enjoyed my holiday but I'm ready to go home now'. They come home and are pleased about the little things that make home ... home. Then, after 10 days back at

work, they're desperate to get away again and start thinking about the next holiday. And what about us Scots in particular? All year long we moan about the weather – too cold, too rainy, miserable grey skies and low cloud. Then after a few days in the sun (and traditional Scottish sunburn) we're moaning about it being too hot! Are people ever going to be happy? How are we going to get happy?

By now you know the kind of answers given by Christians to the questions 'What is being a human all about?' and 'What are we aiming for in life?'. Now let's tackle the last question; 'How do we get it?'.

When we put so much energy into our holidays what are we looking for? An answer?

Probably one of the reasons you're doing RMPS – apart from your probably brilliant teacher of course – is that you like thinking things through for yourself. School pupils in some subjects (which will remain nameless) are much happier with just being told what to write. 'Just tell me the answer Sir!' So far you have thought through what Christians think is wrong with humans and what they should be aiming for – now, how do they get there? Is there an easy answer to this?

Again, different Christian groups have different approaches to the question of how we get what we're meant to from life. There is no one answer, but there are common ideas throughout the Christian faith. Pretty much all Christians think that *the means* are a combination of belief and action. Is Christianity a means to an end or just a means in itself? You're getting closer to the answer as you get nearer to the end of your course. To summarise your course so far let's compare it with you sitting your exams:

The Condition – Your education is incomplete.
The Goals – You want to complete it by passing your exams.
The Means – You'll have to study hard.

As for human life:

The Condition – Humans are apart from God this results in sin and suffering.
The Goals – Getting back into a relationship with God and so escaping from sin and suffering
The Means – Next section . . .

Getting into it

◆ How do you get what you want in life?

◆ What beliefs do you hold?

◆ How central are these beliefs in your life?

◆ How do these beliefs lead to action?

◆ What action?

◆ How public and open are you about what you believe?

◆ Have you ever taken part in or witnessed ceremonies where people demonstrate what they believe?

◆ What kind of world are you helping to create?

◆ What things in life do you think are unfair/unjust?

◆ Do you fight against what you think is unfair/unjust?

◆ What groups are you part of?

◆ How do these groups help you in life?

The Birth of Jesus

Posh and Beckham in wax nativity

Victoria and David Beckham's wax doubles have been given starring roles in a celebrity nativity scene at Madame Tussauds in London.

The pair play Mary and Joseph, while Tony Blair, George Bush and the Duke of Edinburgh make up the three wise men.

Actors Hugh Grant, Samuel L Jackson and comedian Graham Norton play shepherds and singer Kylie Minogue is the angel.

But church leaders are said to be unimpressed. A Vatican spokesman told The Times it was "in very poor taste".

Source:
http://news.bbc.co.uk/2/hi/uk_news/england/london/4078285.stm

Time Out 36

What do you think of this nativity scene? Funny? Blasphemous? Bad taste?

Wakey wakey

Unless you've been asleep in RMPS for the past few years (don't answer) you'll know the story of the birth of Jesus, or the nativity as it's sometimes known. Who knows – maybe in primary school you draped your best bath towel round your head and acted it all out in a nativity play. Everyone knows the story – but does everyone know what it all means?

Christians believe that the story is filled with symbolism and meaning – all pointing to the importance of Jesus as the means of getting humans and God back into their right relationship.

Christian view

Just because we are so comfortably familiar with the story we need to listen very carefully to its message about a God who loves us so much that he sent his Son into our world to tell us what he is like and to show us what he is like. We can all be moved by the awe and wonder with which little children respond to Christmas. As grown-ups we too need to rediscover the wonder at the heart of the Christmas story.

Maxton and Mertoun with St Boswells Church of Scotland Newsletter
http://www.maxton.bordernet.co.uk/church/131.html

Poverty, riches and danger

Talking Point 36

Do you agree that people remember the Christmas story but not the meaning?

Jesus is born in a stable of sorts, there being nowhere else to stay. This happened after a long and difficult journey for a pregnant woman and must have been a bit grim. His first visitors were local shepherds who'd probably been given the fright of their life by an angel telling them to go and see this baby. So Jesus was born in humble surroundings to a working-class family, and his first visitors were ordinary folk. All of this signifies that Jesus has come for the ordinary people. His next visitors are wealthy men from the East – bringing gifts of great value. These powerful men bow before this child – signifying that Jesus is also a powerful person to whom even the rich and powerful will have to pay attention. Not only that, but they have followed a star to his birthplace and have come via a visit to King Herod who has asked them to let him know where this child is once they find him. Herod's worried about this birth. He thinks it means that his place as ruler is threatened – so much so that he orders all male children to be killed. Jesus is not only for the rich and powerful too – but his life is marked by personal danger right at the start. Trouble's obviously going to follow this kid. The men from the East are warned to go home a different way and Jesus and his family are spared.

Of course, some people are a little dubious about the historical truth of this story and a little concerned at the supernatural events surrounding it. Does it sound too much to be true? Once more, Christians have different views. Some believe the story is a literal description of all that happened. Shifting the stars about when you're God isn't exactly difficult. Each element of the story has meaning

Talking Point (37)

How important is it for Christians to believe that the birth story actually happened as described in the Bible?

and plays a small part in the whole tale. Other Christians are happy to accept the story as a way of expressing who Jesus was and what he had come for, but not literally true.

Church of Scotland view

I remember realising for the first time that Christmas was as much about sacrifice as was Easter and as pivotal. The significance of Christ's humanity and God's commitment to his creation is in fact a Christmas story. When we understand the Word made flesh in this way, we understand that the pure and innocent and vulnerable baby of Bethlehem is indeed God with us.

Alison Twaddle, General Secretary of the Church of Scotland Guild
http://www.churchofscotland.org.uk/boards/guild/gdworship1203.htm

See, I told you so ...

An important part of the Jesus birth story is that it was a fulfillment of the prophecies in the Jewish Scriptures (Christian Old Testament). It has been claimed that there are around 300 prophecies in the Old Testament of the first coming of the Messiah, all of them made hundreds of years before the birth of Jesus. Many Christians believe that Jesus fulfilled all of these. George Heron, a French mathematician, calculated that the odds of one man fulfilling only 40 of those prophecies are 1 in 10^{157}. Christians believe that the Old Testament builds towards the coming of the Messiah. The Old Testament is

the record of God trying to re-establish the relationship between himself and his creation. Jesus is also often referred to as Immanuel – God with us. Jesus is the final chapter in that story. Christians believe that Jesus was the Messiah – everything the Old Testament had pointed to. So, the nativity just makes real what the prophecies had already foretold. But hang on ... Some have argued that the people who wrote the New Testament would have known about these

Time Out (37)

Have a look at **www.thetruthmini stry.8k.com/cust om2.html** and look at some of the references for OT prophecies fulfilled in the NT. How strong is all this evidence in supporting the view that the OT points towards Jesus?

prophecies and they would've had them in mind when writing about Jesus' birth. So they would put a 'spin' on the birth story to make it more like a fulfilment of the old prophecies and so make it seem more amazing. This is a bit of a chicken-and-egg issue and different Christians see it differently. But almost all Christians agree that the story of Jesus follows on naturally from the Old Testament stories – otherwise why would these be in the Christian's Bible at all?

The virgin birth issue

For lots of people, the virgin birth is a bit like the Adam and Eve story – a little hard to accept. The Old Testament prophesises that the Messiah will be born of a virgin (Isaiah 7:14). One Bible commentary on this verse says: 'Scarcely any verse in the Bible has been more debated and discussed than this'. The word used here is the Hebrew 'almah' which can mean 'virgin', 'young woman' or both. Some Christians worry that too much time is spent on whether Jesus was conceived in this rather unusual way or not – others think that it is central to the whole question of who Jesus was. Supporters of a virgin birth say the following:

◆ If Jesus had been conceived in the normal way by Mary and Joseph then he would have been completely human. He would have been born inheriting the original sin of Adam and so would have been sinful.

◆ As a result he would not have been able to be a bridge between God and mankind because he'd only be a man.

◆ He had to be completely human and completely God to fulfil the role he was being given and the only way for this to happen was for him to be conceived without the usual human business being involved. This meant also that he was born sinless – as he would remain throughout his life.

Roman Catholic view

The Roman Catholic view that Jesus was born of a virgin is quite clear. It says that:

- The body of Jesus Christ was not sent down from Heaven, nor taken from earth as was that of Adam, but that its matter was supplied by Mary.

- Mary co-operated in the formation of Christ's body as every other mother co-operates in the formation of the body of her child, since otherwise Christ could not be said to be born of Mary, just as Eve cannot be said to be born of Adam.

- The germ, in whose development and growth into the infant Jesus, Mary co-operated, was fecundated not by any human action, but by the Divine power attributed to the Holy Ghost.

Source: http://www.newadvent.org/cathen/15448a.htm

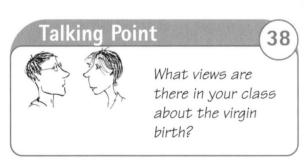

Talking Point (38)

What views are there in your class about the virgin birth?

Other Christians say that he could still have been conceived in the normal human way but then given something special by God which marked him out as more than human. Finally, some Christians say that as a human – however conceived, he was in a way 'God's Son' just like everyone is, and so could still fulfil the special role given to him by God.

Scottish Christian View

This passage tells us how Jesus was born by the action of the Holy Spirit. It tells us of what we call the virgin birth. The virgin birth is a doctrine which presents us with many difficulties, and it is a doctrine which our Church does not compel us to accept in the literal and the physical sense. This is one of the doctrines on which the Church says that we have full liberty to come to our own belief and our own conclusion. Let us leave aside all the doubtful and debatable things, and let us here concentrate on the great birth, as Matthew would wish us to do.

William Barclay, Scottish Theologian, The Gospel of Matthew. pp 10–11.

A unique spirit

So, many Christians argue that Jesus was a unique human being. He had all the qualities of a human but all the qualities of God too – and that was the point. The gospel of John matches Jesus up with something called the divine logos – or word. John says that this logos was there in the beginning and was the same as God and that this word became flesh and dwelt among us (John 1:14). This is what the word incarnation means – literally 'God made flesh' or 'God in human form'. Only by becoming human could God finally get the last chance message through to people. This is the true message of the birth story of Jesus – that God took on a human form to show people the way back to him. Jesus himself was therefore a means by which humans and God could get it right.

Saviour

The first Christians summed up what Jesus was all about in a simple drawing of a fish. The Greek word for fish is 'icthus' and Christians turned this into a natty mnemonic to show what they believed.

I – Iesus – Jesus
C – Christos – the Christ
THeou – of God
Uios – the Son
Sator – Saviour

Christos, or Christ – is just a Greek word which means the same as the Hebrew word Messiah – one sent by God for a specific purpose. Of course, Christians believe that Jesus was *the* Messiah (i.e. the one and only). Saviour is another thing altogether and is the key to what Christians mean by *the means*.

Christians believe that God sent Jesus to save them from their sins – to show them the way to return to him as they should. He loved humans so much that he became one of them and gave them a way out of their sorry condition. A Saviour brings Salvation, and that's the means to achieve everything that's possible in life as a human – for all eternity . . .

Time Out ⑲38

When people talk about someone being their 'saviour', what do they sometimes mean?

Orthodox Christian view

As the Saviour-Messiah, Christ also fulfilled all of the prophecies and expectations of the Old Testament, fulfilling and crowning in final and absolute perfection all that was begun in Israel for human and cosmic salvation. Thus, Christ is the fulfilment of the promise to Abraham, the completion of the Law of Moses, the fulfilment of the prophets and Himself the Final Prophet, the King and the Teacher, the one Great High Priest of Salvation and the Perfect Sacrificial Victim, the New Passover and the Bestower of the Holy Spirit upon all creation.

Source: http://www.fatheralexander.org/booklets/english/christian_doctrine_ext_e.htm

Activities

Knowledge, Understanding, Evaluation

1 Why might a Christian have found the wax nativity offensive?

2 Why might a Christian have been happy with the wax nativity?

3 Describe in outline form the story of the birth of Jesus.

4 Choose three of the symbols in the story. Explain what they mean.

5 What does the word Immanuel mean?

6 Why was Herod keen to find the baby Jesus?

7 What two explanations are there for the fact that the birth story of Jesus closely matches many Old Testament prophecies?

8 Why might some people find the idea of a virgin birth difficult to accept?

9 Summarise the Roman Catholic position on the virgin birth.

10 What is the view of William Barclay on the virgin birth?

11 What does the word incarnation mean?

12 What does the Gospel of John mean by the logos?

13 How does a fish sum up Christian belief about Jesus?

14 What is understood by the word Messiah?

15 What do Christians mean when they call Jesus 'Saviour'?

16 Why is the birth of Jesus important for a Christian?

17 How do the symbols associated with Jesus' birth contribute to the power of the story?

18 How could it help the human/God relationship for God to become human?

Practical Activities

1. The waxworks nativity caused some controversy. Imagine you had to use today's 'heroes' to make up a nativity scene. Who would you use? How would you ensure that people weren't offended? (Could you ensure this?)

2. Draw up a table of symbols in the birth story of Jesus showing what each symbol represents.

3. Design a brief information leaflet on the virgin birth. This should explain different Christian understandings of the virgin birth.

4. Find examples of the nativity story in artwork. Choose a few examples and explain how the message of the nativity is conveyed by different artists. See **www.makedisciples.com/Christmas/ art.htm** for some examples or type 'The birth story of Jesus in art' into a search engine.

5. Make up your own mnemonic to explain the importance of the birth of Jesus using one of the words in the text (e.g. Saviour).

Unit Assessment Question

I1 Explain two symbols associated with the birth of Jesus.   (2KU, 4AE)

Sample Exam Question

I1 'For a Christian it is important to believe that Jesus was born of a virgin'. Explain two ways a Christian might respond to this statement.   (2KU, 4AE)

Homework

Find an example of a Christian hymn which is sung about the birth of Jesus. How does this hymn explain the significance of Jesus' birth?

Personal Reflection

Do you think people's experience of Christmas would benefit from a better understanding of the birth story of Jesus?

Salvation, Baptism and Eucharist

This is a bit funny. One minute I'm lying in my cot all snuggly, the next I'm strapped in the car bumping along headed who knows where. Out we get, Dad picks me up and holds me up against him. Oh oh ... too much milk this morning, too much jiggling in the car ... sicky burp coming up ... bleugh ... Dad's wearing his best suit too. I won't be popular. Strange old building this, I don't remember it. Mind you, I was only born two months ago ... It smells a bit like my soaked nappies. Some of these people will have long memories though. I really don't like the way they press their faces up

against mine breathing all over me ... some of them could do with an extra strong mint by the way ... still, they seem to think I'm a bit special. I like that – other babies I know do too ... There's a lot of people here and then a terrible noise ... how can you expect me not to bawl – a woman is pressing keys on a board and the sound is all around – scary. Oooh it's stopped now. I didn't like that. Mum and Dad have stood up and they're giving me away to a man. He's all in black and smells of dust. He wanders round the building with me showing me to everyone and they look all googly-eyed. He takes me over to a bath. He's going to give me a bath in front of all these people – surely not! I think I'll bawl again – but this time ... seriously. No, he's not going to bath me. He takes some water and makes a tickly mark on my forehead – some of the water runs down my nose and makes me want to sneeze. He gives me a name ... I thought I had one already ... I start to feel all tingly – hope I'm not going to make any rude noises in front of all these people – how embarrassing

Talking Point 39

Have you ever attended the baptism of a baby?

would that be? Suddenly everyone starts singing, and he takes me round everyone again and they all smile at me. I get the feeling that I'm part of this gang now. There's a few other babies there, slightly older than me. All they say in babyish is 'welcome' …

Baptising baby

So who knows what goes through a baby's mind during a baptism ceremony? Baptism is a ceremony carried out in most Christian Churches. It can either be done when you are a baby when it is sometimes called a christening – or when you are an adult when it's called believer's baptism. The ceremonies vary greatly across different Christian groups but all involve some kind of ritual washing with water or sometimes oil. In infant baptism there are special meanings attached to the ceremony – all related to the idea of Salvation.

◆ Baptism ritually washes away original sin which everyone is born with. The water purifies the baby from it's 'contamination' with the sin of Adam. Some Christians think this offers a kind of 'protection' for the baby from bad things happening – though this is really more superstition than Christian belief.

◆ Baptism welcomes the child into the Christian community. One of the benefits of being a Christian is that you're part of God's Kingdom here on earth – remember that your eternal life has already started once you're part of God's Kingdom. So, baptism kicks off a baby's share in the eternal life business.

◆ In infant baptism all the promises are made on behalf of the baby by its parents. This shows that baptism is also about their forgiveness and their repenting the bad things they have done – after all, babies haven't had much time to do anything bad yet – unless you count throwing up on Dad's best suit. Perhaps the parents are also saying sorry for all the sins the baby/child/young adult is about to do?

◆ Even at an infant baptism, the ceremony represents the beginning of a new life – this time one lived as a Christian.

Many Christians think baptising babies is wrong because baptism has to be something you choose for yourself, but for Christians who follow it they argue that the choice is made for the baby by the parents just like they make choices for their children for years to come. Besides, in churches where infants are baptised there are often ceremonies later in life, like confirmation, where those who were baptised confirm for themselves that they accept the 'terms' under which their parents had them baptised.

There is also some difference of opinion about baptising babies whose parents aren't really Christians. In the Church of Scotland in particular – where every home is within a parish – some people have their baby baptised but are not church attenders – nor plan to be. Some Ministers refuse to do these baptisms, others will do them in the hope that it will bring new people into the church – or because they think it's not for them to judge. At an infant baptism the parents promise to accept the Christian faith and bring the child up in a Christian way. Should you agree to something that you don't plan to do?

Church of Scotland view

The Church of Scotland practices both infant and adult baptism. Here's what Meldrum and Bourtie Parish Church's website says about infant baptism:

> As one of the two sacraments of the church Baptism is a symbol of God's grace and forgiveness. It is an outward sign which corresponds to its inward meaning. The sprinkled water carries with it the meaning of cleansing and it directs that promise to the child who is baptised. Baptism is also a sign of our fellowship with Jesus, acknowledging that your child has a place in Jesus' heart and in His Church. It is our prayer that, in time, your child will him/herself choose to follow Christ and to profess the faith in which they were baptised.

Source: http://www.jesusforme.org/meldrum/baptism.htm

Adult (believer's) baptism

Time Out 39

Should Ministers refuse to baptise children whose parents are not regular church attenders?

Many Christians think this is the only realistic form of baptism. Such Christians also think it's important to welcome a baby into the church community so they often have a naming and welcoming ceremony instead of a christening. Jesus was baptised as an adult when he could make his own decision – but he had also been welcomed into the Jewish faith through his circumcision.

Believer's baptism also takes different forms – from sprinkling water to full dunking (or immersion) in a small pool (or sometimes a river or even the sea). This signifies in a very dramatic way that the person has 'died' to their old self and is now 'born again' as a Christian. Supporters of adult baptism believe the following:

◆ It's more meaningful because the person has made a free choice to accept the Christian faith. So, they have exercised their God-given freedom just like Adam did and just like Jesus did – but like Jesus – they have said yes to God.

◆ This acceptance of Jesus is a better outward sign that the person has chosen to be saved from the effects of sin – original and any other kind – than infant baptism, because it is a free choice. Not only that but the person understands what's going on and how significant it all is.

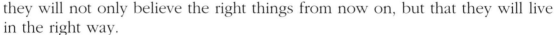

◆ It's also better because the person can now consciously choose to live a more Christian life following their 'rebirth' – so showing that they will not only believe the right things from now on, but that they will live in the right way.

So baptism is the outward sign that you have been saved – so let's now get a final grip on what that means.

A baptist view

There is no one distinctive baptist belief! Baptists are not the only Christians to practise believer's baptism.

On the basis of the New Testament, Baptists claim that baptism is for believers only. Baptism is only for those who are able to declare: 'Jesus is Lord'. As a symbol of Jesus' claim on their lives, Baptists practise baptism by 'immersion', in which candidates symbolise their desire to 'die to self' and to live for Christ.

Baptist Union of Scotland quoted at *www.scottishchristian.com/churches/baptist.shtml*

Salvation

All through this book has been the idea that humans and God are not in the relationship they should be, but God doesn't want to force people to accept him. So he sent Jesus to lead the way back to God. If we accept Jesus – what he taught, how he lived and who he was – then we are saved. In other words we're back to where we're meant to be with God and so sin, death and suffering are things of the past. Our eternal life begins now. In short, the Christian message is that Jesus Saves. How?

Time Out ④⓪

Discuss and record what people in your class think are the advantages and disadvantages of infant baptism compared to believer's baptism.

◆ Jesus was the lamb of God. He was sacrificed for human wrongdoings. In this way he took the place of humanity, standing in for them and taking the punishment – like someone doing an almighty punishment exercise for you as a way of showing you how they feel about you.

◆ The blood of Jesus was shed to pay the price of sin. In this way, our sins were washed away and we could all choose to start off fresh, once we had accepted Jesus. This makes us redeemed (literally 'bought back') and is what Christians mean when they talk about 'redemption'. Jesus' blood could wash away sin because he was born without sin and didn't sin during his life.

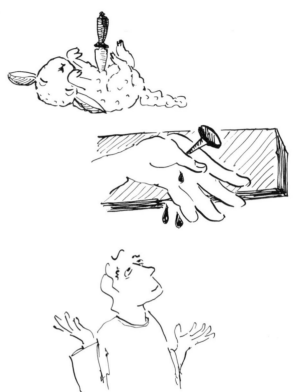

◆ Jesus accepted God's will right up to and including his death. Compare this with Adam who couldn't even be bothered to accept God's will about not eating a bit of fruit. If we accept Jesus, then we accept God's will in the same way.

All of this leads to what Christians call the Atonement. When you atone for something you make up for something which is wrong and you put it right. Jesus atoned for the sin of Adam by canceling his rather duff mistake and setting a new pattern for human/God relationships. This meant that God and mankind can be *at-one* again – a rather nifty play on the word atonement really.

Christian views

The Christian Institute, based in Edinburgh, sees itself as a 'Christian Influence in a Secular World'. It believes in:

> Salvation from the guilt, penalty and all other consequences of sin solely through the work of Jesus Christ – his perfect obedience, substitutionary death, bodily resurrection and exaltation as Lord. He alone is truly God and truly man, the only mediator between God and man. There is salvation through no other person, creed, process or power. Each sinner is justified before God and reconciled to him only by his grace appropriated through faith alone.

Source: http://www.christianscotland.org/introduction/basisoffaith.htm

The Roman Catholic Church suggests that the Church itself is part of what it means to be saved:

> 824 United with Christ, the Church is sanctified by him; through him and with him she becomes sanctifying. 'All the activities of the Church are directed, as toward their end, to the sanctification of men in Christ and the glorification of God.' It is in the Church that 'the fullness of the means of salvation' has been deposited. It is in her that 'by the grace of God we acquire holiness.'
>
> *Source: Catholic Catechism at www.vatican.va/archive/ENG0015/__P29.HTM*

Can anyone be saved?

Talking Point 40

Look back to your work in Talk Point 15 on page 40. Have any of your views changed now that you're at this point in the course?

Easy answer: Yes. As Jesus was on the cross a criminal being crucified alongside him asked him for forgiveness. Jesus told him he'd be with him in paradise soon. Being saved is just a simple matter of free choice, nothing more. Following this free choice it's living a life which matches the decision you've made. It's not always going to be easy for Christians because they still have to live in a fallen world where most people have not chosen to be saved, but there you go. Lots of changes to your life will follow being saved but the actual saving is simplicity itself – you just say yes to God.

The sacraments

One way in which most Christians demonstrate that they have accepted Jesus is by taking part in the sacraments. The sacraments are believed to be outward visible signs of God's love for mankind. When you take part in a sacrament you are taking part in something which mysteriously links you to God and shows that you have accepted God's will and are now getting the benefits of that.

One important sacrament which almost all Christians take part in is Eucharist/Communion. Again, there are more ways of celebrating this than you can shake a stick at, but all involve some kind of re-enactment of the last supper Jesus had with his disciples before the events of his death and Resurrection really got going. All involve bread and wine – whether it's hovis and buckfast or mother's pride and ribena. These remember the body of Christ which died for us and his blood which was shed for us. Consuming these things helps you both remember the events and somehow gives you a 'taste' of what Jesus was all about. Roman Catholic faith teaches that the bread and wine become the actual body and blood of Jesus. This is called transubstantiation – most other Christian churches don't accept this. They prefer to think that the elements of bread and wine are just symbols of the body and blood of Jesus and stay bread and wine throughout your digestive process. But this points to the central idea that sharing in the sacraments has an element of mystery. Somehow you get the benefits of being a Christian here but it's not really necessary to go into the fine details of it all. Like baptism, Eucharist has a few dimensions:

◆ It's an outward sign of your faithfulness in accepting Jesus – and so rubber stamps your faith and all the benefits of having it.

◆ It's a remembrance of what Jesus went through for you – so sometimes it's very solemn.

◆ It's a celebration of what Jesus means, and so sometimes it's a big party (the word Eucharist itself suggests thanks-giving and celebration).

◆ It's a way of renewing the bond between you and God – that's why some Christian groups call it Communion.

◆ But it's also a way of strengthening your link with fellow Christians as you share this experience with them on a fairly regular basis.

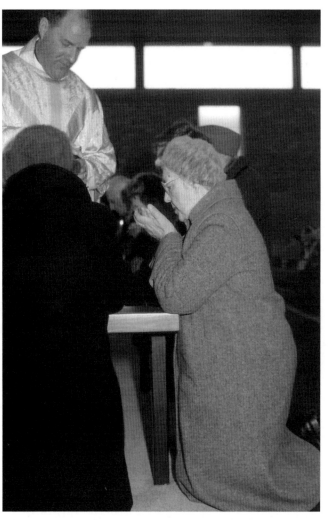

Christian views

In the Orthodox Church, Eucharist is central:

> The Holy Eucharist is called the 'sacrament of sacraments' in the Orthodox tradition. Everything in the Church leads to the Eucharist, and all things flow from it. It is the completion of all of the Church's sacraments – the source and the goal of all of the Church's doctrines and institutions. The Passover meal was transformed by Christ into an act done in remembrance of him: of his life, death and resurrection as the new and eternal Passover Lamb who frees men from the slavery of evil, ignorance and death and transfers them into the everlasting life of the Kingdom of God.
>
> *Source: www.oca.org/pages/orth_chri/Orthodox-Faith/Worship/Holy-Eucharist.html*

The Communion Table in the Church of Scotland is open to all who Love the Lord and an invitation to that effect is usually given prior to a Communion Service. Indeed the act that affirms Children at Communion states this:

> 'The Lord's Table is open to any baptised person who Loves the Lord and responds in faith to the invitation to "Take, eat"'.
>
> *Source: http://www.kirkweb.org/ministry.htm*

> It is the primary duty of parents and guardians and of the priest to ensure that children who have reached the age of reason (about seven years of age) are properly prepared for the reception of the sacrament as soon as possible. Parishes arrange a period of preparation, both for children and parents. During the course of preparation numerous liturgies, in addition to the classes, take place so as to enable the child to grow in the love of Jesus Christ whose body he or she will receive for the first time. It is the duty of the priest to see that children who have not reached the age of reason or who are insufficiently disposed do not come to Holy Communion.
>
> *Source: http://www.catholic.org.uk/library/basics/fhc.shtml*

Now what?

Once a Christian is saved and shows it through taking part in the outward signs of being saved, what next? Is it enough to keep turning up in church and doing the religious ceremony stuff? Most Christians don't think so. You can't create the Kingdom of God on earth just by sitting at home or going to church … can you?

Talking Point   **41**

At what age should you be allowed to take part in the Eucharist/ Communion?

Activities

Knowledge, Understanding, Evaluation

1 What usually happens at the baptism of a baby?

2 Do you think it is right to baptise a baby even though it can't agree to it happening?

3 Why do you think a baptism is sometimes called a christening?

4 What things might someone believe baptism does for a baby?

5 What role do the baby's parents play in baptism?

6 What is confirmation all about?

7 According to the Church of Scotland, what is the meaning of baptism?

8 Does the fact that Jesus was baptised as an adult mean that Christians should wait until they are adults to be baptised? Explain your answer.

9 For some Christians, adult baptism is the only meaningful baptism. Why?

10 Describe in what way an adult baptism might be different from an infant baptism.

11 What do you have to be able to declare to undergo baptism in the Baptist Church?

12 In what way does baptism show that you have been saved?

13 In what way might a Christian think of baptism as an outward sign of God's grace?

14 Explain two ways in which Christians think 'Jesus Saves'.

15 What does the word 'atonement' mean?

16 What does the Christian Institute think the role of Jesus is in saving people?

17 What role does the Roman Catholic Church think the Church plays in you being saved?

18 What two things does a Christian have to do to be saved?

19 What do Christians understand by a sacrament?

20 What do all Eucharist celebrations have in common?

21 Why might a Christian take part in the Eucharist?

22 Why is the Eucharist equally well-known as Communion?

23 What evidence is there that the Eucharist is central to the Orthodox Christian faith?

24 Who can take part in Communion in the Church of Scotland?

25 When are Roman Catholics first allowed to take Communion?

26 In your opinion what are the benefits for a Christian in taking part in the Eucharist/Communion?

Practical Activities

1 Find out how baptism is actually carried out in two different Christian Churches. Half of the class should focus on infant baptism and half on adult baptism. This is a group task. Prepare an illustrated report on your findings.

2 Based on what you have studied so far in this course on Christianity, think about the preparations someone will have to go through before being baptised. Write the outline of a course in Christianity for people about to be baptised. At the end of this think of five questions which should be asked of an adult or the parents of a child just before the person (or the child) is baptised.

3 Find out how Eucharist is celebrated in two or three different Christian churches. Make a class display about this. Perhaps you could also design a new (alternative?) way to celebrate Eucharist.

4 If you're in a Roman Catholic school, devise an A4 information sheet for pupils in a non-denominational school about first Communion in the Catholic Church. If you're in a non-denominational school, devise a questionnaire about a Catholic's first Communion. Then get in touch with the nearest RC/Non-D school and exchange these – learn from each other!

Unit Assessment Question

I1 What do Christians mean by salvation?   (3KU)

I2 Explain what a Christian means by the phrase 'Jesus saves'.   (4KU, 2AE)

Higher

Explain how a Christian might achieve Salvation.   (8)

Sample Exam Question

I1 Describe what happens at a typical Christian baptism.   (6KU)

I2 How might a Christian support the view that adult baptism is more meaningful than infant baptism?   (2KU, 4AE)

Higher

'To be considered Christian, you must be baptised.'

How far would a Christian agree?   (4 KU, 6 AE)

Homework

The Salvation Army motto is 'Blood and Fire'. Find out what this means and explain why it is an appropriate motto for this Christian group.

Personal Reflection

How would your life change if you 'got saved'?

Justice, Community and Kingdom

Sit back and imagine this possible world:

This is a world where everyone is treated fairly. Where people get paid for their efforts. Where it doesn't matter whether you are black or white. Where men and women are treated as equals. Where there is no violence – not even angry words. Where religious differences are celebrated – not treated with suspicion. Where all parents and teachers treat children with respect – and where children give the same respect back. Where age-old disagreements are forgotten. Where no-one is hungry for power – and no-one is hungry. Where those who are ill are treated for free – without the worry of how to pay for it. Where everyone's opinion matters. Where no-one is bullied or made to feel unimportant. Where everyone is valued for who they are. Where love for your fellow humanity is the most prized treasure.

Now think of one thing you could do today to start off a world like this.

> ## Talking Point (42)
> *Why do most people in your class probably think that such a world is impossible?*

What do Christians mean by justice?

For Christians and probably you too, Justice means what an Australian might talk about as 'fair dinkum'. This just means fair and square – maximum respect. Justice is how things should be – everyone doing and getting what's right. For

Discuss in class – When did you last put someone's needs before yours? Is it something you do a lot or only in certain situations?

Christians, Justice is something they want to make real in the world – for everyone. It has two sides – a side you contribute to and a side you benefit from. If everyone behaved in a just way towards everyone else then the world would be a pretty amazing place, because you would always put other people first – imagine …

Christian views on justice

The Church of Scotland is one of the largest Social Care organisations in Scotland. It says:

> The Church of Scotland aims to worship God by following the teachings of Jesus Christ. We express our love for God by our love and practical care for each other and for those we live with and encounter in our daily lives.
>
> *Source: www.churchofscotland.org.uk/spirituality/spiritaims.htm*

The Roman Catholic Catechism states:

1943 Society ensures social justice by providing the conditions that allow associations and individuals to obtain their due.

1944 Respect for the human person considers the other 'another self'. It presupposes respect for the fundamental rights that flow from the dignity intrinsic of the person.

1945 The equality of men concerns their dignity as persons and the rights that flow from it.

1946 The differences among persons belong to God's plan, who wills that we should need one another. These differences should encourage charity.

1947 The equal dignity of human persons requires the effort to reduce excessive social and economic inequalities. It gives urgency to the elimination of sinful inequalities.

Source: www.vatican.va/archive/ENG0015/__P6R.HTM

The Salvation Army is one of the best-known Christian organisations which puts social care into action. It has even been referred to as 'Christianity with its sleeves rolled up'. Its mission statement is:

We will be a Spirit-filled, radical, growing movement with a burning desire to:

◆ lead people into a saving knowledge of Jesus Christ;

◆ actively serve the community;

◆ fight for social justice.

Source: www.salvationarmy.org.uk/en/Mission+Statement.htm

What does justice involve in practice?

Peace. – This doesn't just mean no war, but active peace – not an uneasy truce (though maybe that would do to be going on with). War has consequences – all of them grim ones. Preparing for war takes time, effort and energy – all of which could be going into something much more positive. The cost of one fighter aircraft for example could support a family in the developing world for a lifetime and a bit. Being at war destroys lives – of those who die obviously, but also of those who are left behind. And the effects of war go on – sometimes in grudges and acts of revenge for years to come sometimes in the remains of weapons like landmines – ready to harm long after war is over. As well as a practical thing, peace is an attitude of

mind. It means compromising with people you disagree with – and living with them despite your differences – maybe even getting to like them!

Equality – Male/female; rich/poor; black/white; Scottish/English. Equality means being treated for who you are, not because of a difference in race, gender, skin colour, social class etc. It means accepting people who are different to you – showing that you think they are just as important to you as you are to yourself! Equality means that everyone gets out of life what they put into it and that your life isn't a game of chance which depends upon you having been born in the right place at the right time with the right skin colour or accent.

Talking Point 43

What's stopping the world being a more just place?

Fairness – This means getting what you deserve and being rewarded for what you have done. 'It's not fair!' is something we've all said at some point in our life, but you have to make sure that you didn't just mean 'I don't like this so it's not fair'. When something's truly not fair is when there is a mis-match between what you get and what you deserve.

All of these can be grouped under the bigger heading of 'justice'. A just world is where all of these things are balanced and in harmony which is probably why justice is often represented as a set of scales.

Why are Christians so interested in justice?

Justice is central to the message of the Christian faith. Everything and everyone is God's creation. Christians believe that because we all belong to God we all deserve the best. When we don't get the best that's injustice. Christians believe that it is their job to make sure that all God's creation gets what it deserves – justice. For this reason, Christians try to create a just world which is the kind of world God wants there to be. This is known as the Kingdom of God. Christians believe that creating such a world will make the world now like a taster of what's to come in Eternal Life. Here there will be peace, equality, fairness and everything will be living in harmony – all getting back to exactly what it should be. The letter of Paul to the Church in Galatia spoke about this when it said that there was, 'neither Jew nor Gentile, male nor female … for all are one in Christ Jesus'. Christians believe that living the kind of life Jesus set as an example will lead to a world of fairness – God's Kingdom. Jesus spent a lot of his time teaching people about justice:

◆ **Luke 6:27–35** – You should love people no matter who they are. It's easy to care for people you like – it's the ones you don't like that it's hard to love. You shouldn't do this for reward from them – but you will get a reward from God – the greatest kind. Do you show love to all?

◆ **Luke 15:11–31** – Remember the story of the prodigal son? Justice involves forgiveness and loving a person no matter what they have done if they ask for your forgiveness. How forgiving are you?

Time Out 42

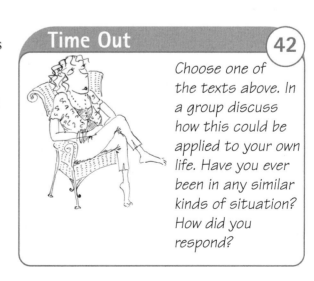

Choose one of the texts above. In a group discuss how this could be applied to your own life. Have you ever been in any similar kinds of situation? How did you respond?

◆ **Luke 18:18–19** – In today's world, justice is often closely linked to how you use your wealth. Spending power is something most people in Scotland have – do you spend your money in a way which will create a just world?

◆ **Luke 7:1–10** – Jesus healed the servant of an enemy soldier. Justice means responding to people's needs – no matter who they are. Do you help some more than others?

The Christian community in action

Christian Aid seeks to create God's Kingdom on earth here and now. Christian Aid works to publicise the plight of those who are poor and suffering the effects of injustice, but it also carries out direct action to help such people improve their lives. It doesn't just give handouts – it helps people to stand on their own feet and take control of their own lives, and it doesn't just help Christians. It believes that people should be helped no matter who they are if they are in need – after all, that's the fairest way. Christian Aid raises money here in the UK to do its work both here and in other areas of need

in the world. Christian Aid began as a collection of Christian Churches working together to help the needy. The Catholic Organisation CAFOD works in a similar way to Christian Aid. CAFOD has, as one of its mottoes, 'It's time for Justice'. TEARFUND too works in a similar way to both these organisations and is based on an Evangelical approach to Christianity. TEARFUND's website says simply; 'Tearfund works through local churches and Christian agencies – our partners – to open up brighter futures for the world's poorest communities. Together we're helping people become all that God wants them to be.' (***www.tearfund.org.***)

Talking Point (44)

Should you give money to a Christian organisation if you are not a Christian?

Of course, most people are aware of large-scale organisations such as these, but there are other Christian groups working to create the Kingdom of God too – sometimes in a smaller, quieter way but just as effectively:

◆ The Bethany Christian Trust in Edinburgh helps rehabilitate those who have been made homeless, often as a result of drug or substance abuse. Its website

describes its work as simply 'an expression of Christianity'.
(***www.bethanychristiantrust.com***).

◆ Church Action on Poverty aims to help those in poverty and make others aware of poverty issues. It says: 'Church Action on Poverty believes that the Gospel calls on us to stand alongside those for whom poverty is their daily living experience. We believe that people with direct experience of poverty are the real "poverty experts".'
(***www.church-poverty.org.uk/_html/aboutus.htm***).

◆ A Christian group, Emmaus helps the homeless and has a major branch in Glasgow. Its President is Terry Waite, a Christian who was kidnapped in Lebanon and held hostage for many years. The organisation states that it's 'Giving people a bed … and a reason to get out of it'.
(***www.emmausglasgow.org.uk***).

A cup of tea and a sticky bun

The organisations above are large well-organised groups which work almost like businesses but without the profit. Ordinary Christians can also help create the Kingdom of God in their own way by bringing about justice on a much smaller scale. The Christian Community not only means UK-wide professional organisations, it's also single churches, groups and individuals within a church. In fact, most Christians will argue that the Church is not a building or an

organisation – it's the people in it. These people make up the Christian community, and it's their actions which go towards creating the Kingdom of God on earth. Running a mother and toddler's group or a summer play scheme, or a youth group or providing a cup of tea and a sticky bun can all help bring about a world of justice – giving people a taste of what God's Kingdom is all about.

Talking Point 45

Should schools have chaplains?

Even school chaplaincy groups explaining their beliefs to challenging teenagers is a way of creating a world of justice. You might not agree with what they say but don't you have a right to hear it anyway?

Individual action

You don't need to team up with other Christians – what you do on your own is just as meaningful – and after all, most organisations start with one or two individuals getting together and it grows from there (remember the parable of the mustard seed?). Individual Christian action can change the world – or even just a little corner of it, but it's a start.

Oscar Romero

Oscar was the Roman Catholic Archbishop of San Salvador. He lived at a time of the development of Liberation Theology – a view among Catholics in South America which believed that before you could preach the faith you had to feed the poor and free the oppressed. Romero was wary of the whole movement. But as more of his own priests were killed for standing up for the oppressed he eventually came to favour the approach. He worked tirelessly for the poor – helping them to improve their lives but also speaking out against the politics which kept them poor. His protests were always peaceful and he remained loyal to the Church hierarchy while living and working amongst the poor. In 1980 he was assassinated while saying mass.

George MacLeod

George was a Church of Scotland Minster in Glasgow. In 1938 he began work restoring the Abbey on Iona and setting up a community of Christians who would put social action into practice in the world. From small beginnings, the Iona Community is now a world-wide community of Christians with common purpose and approaches to the Christian life which is committed to:

'rebuilding the common life, through working for social and political change, striving for the renewal of the church with an ecumenical emphasis, and exploring new more inclusive approaches to worship, all based on an integrated understanding of spirituality' (***www.iona.org.uk/community/main.htm***).

Each member of the Community follows a rule which involves:

◆ daily prayer and reading the Bible;

◆ mutual accountability for their use of time and money;

◆ regular meetings together;

◆ action and reflection for justice, peace and the integrity of creation.

Members of the Iona Community are committed to ensuring that there is justice in the world. The Community rule develops the idea further by saying that:

'everyone should have the quality and dignity of a full life that requires adequate physical, social and political opportunity, without the oppression of poverty, injustice and fear'.

Jackie Pullinger

Jackie was just an ordinary girl who wanted to do something meaningful with her life. She arrived in Hong Kong in 1966 and was immediately drawn to its most notorious and dangerous city, Kowloon's Walled City. She felt as if God was calling her to this place. Here, drug addicts, prostitutes and violent gang members were helped by Jackie to become Christians and turn their lives around. It was, and still is, dangerous and difficult work but Jackie's still there. See ***www.ststephenssociety.org/current_work/index.htm*** for some details of Jackie's current work.

Moving in mysterious ways

Many people who are dubious about Christianity claim that there's not much proof of God being around or doing very much. Christians would disagree. According to them the world that God wants – and which is best for us – is being created all around you. It's being done by the Christian community whether that's big organisations, small churches or even someone with a teapot in their hand. Christians believe that one of the features of being a Christian is letting God work through you. By living a Christian life individual Christians are creating a just world – God's Kingdom on Earth. So, from all that you have studied so far, you are able to reflect on the human condition, goals and means of achieving those goals in life. For Christians this means:

◆ Christians know what's wrong with human life.

◆ They know what human life should ideally be like.

◆ They know how to make this happen.

That's what the Christian faith is all about. What do you think?

Activities

Knowledge, Understanding, Evaluation

1 How possible is the ideal world on page 116?

2 What kinds of things do people in your class think they could do to start off an ideal world such as this?

3 How does the Church of Scotland aim to express its love for God?

4 According to the Roman Catholic Church, what should differences encourage?

5 What does it call inequalities?

6 How does the Salvation Army fight for social justice?

7 In what way is peace an element of justice?

8 Why would a Christian think that equality is important?

9 What does a Christian mean by the Kingdom of God?

10 How can a Christian work to create the Kingdom of God?

11 Describe one teaching of Jesus on justice.

12 Describe the work of one Christian organisation which works for justice in the world.

13 Why do these organisations do what they do?

14 Should a Christian organisation help people who aren't Christians? Explain your view.

15 In what ways can ordinary Christians work for justice?

16 What did Oscar Romero do to work for justice?

17 What did George MacLeod's work lead to?

18 How did Jackie Pullinger put her Christian faith into action?

19 What does a Christian mean by saying that God can work through people?

20 What do you think of Christianity's view of humans, its goals and its means?

Practical Activities

1 Carry out further research into a Christian organisation which works for justice. Then examine the area in which you live. What could a Christian organisation do best to help people in your area?

2 Think through the idea of an ideal world. Complete a table with three

columns as shown below. An example has been given for you.

3 Turn one of the teachings of Jesus on pages 119–20 into a drama with a message. You could perform this at an assembly.

4 Find a Christian in your local community who is working to create

the Kingdom of God. Write a series of questions you'd like to ask this person – perhaps you could invite him/her in to school – or better still go visit and lend a hand.

5 Prepare a Fact File on a Christian who works/has worked for justice. This could be someone world famous or the person you linked up with in the previous activity.

Problem	What it should be	How can it be solved?
Homelessness	People having homes	People who have spare rooms in their house offer to take in a homeless person.

Unit Assessment Question

I1 Describe three ways in which a Christian can show concern for others   (6KU)

I2 Describe how one Christian has put justice into action   (4KU)

Higher

'Christians *must* be involved in social action.'

How far would a Christian agree?   (10)

Sample Exam Question

I1 Why is the idea of justice important to Christians?   (2KU, 2AE)

I2 Why would a Christian want to help others?   (4AE)

Higher

In what ways can Christians create the Kingdom of God?   (6 KU)

Homework

Look through one newspaper. Find an example of what Christians might call injustice and suggest how a Christian individual or group could help.

Personal Reflection

Could you do more to help others? Should you? Will you?

Textual Sources

Hebrews 2: 9–10

This passage picks up an idea from Psalm 8, showing that Jesus was made human so that God could become flesh and suffer and die to pay off the debt of sin. Through this suffering and death, Jesus is exalted back to his heavenly status – showing that humans can be too if they share in the experience of Jesus. The whole reasons for Jesus' earthly existence is summed up in this passage – he completed the relationship between God and man by turning it back to what it should have been originally. By doing this he gives humans another chance to say yes to God. If they do, they return to full relationship with God and all the benefits of that. Jesus gives humans a way back to God – a way to overcome death and suffering and a way to be saved from themselves and the effects of sin.

Hebrews 2: 14–18

Again this stresses the importance of Jesus becoming human. By overcoming death he robs the devil of his power (remember he let death in after persuading Adam and Eve to eat the forbidden fruit). Freedom from fear of death is recognised here as a big problem for humans – something which tied them down throughout their lives. Jesus frees them from death – so he frees them from the fear of death and also the guilt of sin. It is stated again that Jesus makes payment for the sins of people. The High Priests of ancient Israel made offerings to God to look kindly on people – even though they were sinful. Jesus becomes like this high priest, but even more – he becomes an ordinary person, sharing in every human experience. Only in this way can he understand, and so conquer, sin and death.

Hebrews 9: 25–26

In the Old Testament, the High Priest entered the Holy of Holies every year to carry out a sacred ritual to make up for the sins of the past year. He did this through sacrificing an animal and offering its blood as a way of saying sorry for all the sins committed by the people during the year. This passage suggests that there is no need for Jesus to die repeatedly – his blood sacrifice washes away sin and is a once-and-for-all event.

1 Corinthians 11: 23–24

This passage picks up the story of the Last Supper as found in Matthew 26:26–28, Mark 14:22–24 and Luke 22:17–19. These are the words of Jesus and now the basis for all Eucharist ceremonies within the Christian faith. Jesus commanded people to continue this meal as a celebration and remembrance of what he was all about. This wasn't just to be remembered though, it was to be *done*. The breaking of bread and drinking of wine symbolise the breaking of his body and the shedding of his blood as the means of salvation.

Acts 2: 38–42

Peter reminds the first Christians that they have to turn from their old sinful ways to a new birth. They had to give up or repent their old actions. Baptism itself didn't save them – their repentance did. Baptism was just the outward sign of the inner change of heart and rebirth. Anyone can share in these benefits because Christ came for all mankind. By being baptised and living the new style of life which it implies, Christians can be saved from the negative effects of living in a fallen world. Following their repentance and baptism the Christians shared fellowship – living in close community and supporting each other through their beliefs and actions.

Textual work

The following is the kind of question you may meet in your RMPS exam. NB: Remember, there are no prescribed sources at Intermediate 1.

Read the following source then answer all parts of the question (a)–(e). The number of marks available for each part is indicated, use them to help you answer the question.

1 Corinthians 11: 23–24

(a) Which event does this passage refer to?
(4 marks) *KU*

(b) Describe how the Eucharist ceremony is carried out in one Christian tradition.
(6 marks) *KU*

(c) Explain two Christian understandings of the role of the bread and wine in the Eucharist.
(6 marks) *(4KU, 2AE)*

(d) 'A Christian can only be true to his faith if he takes part in regular celebrations of the Eucharist.'
Is this true? Explain your answer with reference to two Christian traditions. *(6 marks)*
(8 marks) *(4KU, 4AE)*

(e) Should the Eucharist ceremony be modernised?
(6 marks) *AE*

Revision and Study Guide

What's this course been for?

This has not been a course intended to turn you into a Christian. It's been a way of helping you understand more about one of the most influential faiths in the history of the world. You should now be able to appreciate Christianity a bit more even if you don't agree with any of it at all. Hopefully, in studying the course, you will have had some kind of chance to further explore what you *do* think about the beliefs and practices you've studied. Apart from that you'll be able to sort out the gold from the gloop. How many times have you looked for something on the internet only to discover that there are a zillion trillion websites about that topic – aaargh! How do you know what's a Christian viewpoint and what is just some loopy guy sitting at his computer making up 'Christian' beliefs? You should also be better placed to spot a genuine Christian belief and better able to spot the chancers and the frauds – or those who claim to be Christian and have some weird and unfortunately not wonderful ideas which they'd like you to share ... So you'll know about Christian beliefs but you'll also be in a good position to evaluate them too.

More than 57 varieties

Remember that Christianity is a very wide and varied religion – it is very difficult to end a sentence which begins 'Christians believe ...' because there are so many different Christian viewpoints. Some Christians won't accept everything that's written in this book – everyone's entitled to their opinion, but that's partly what it's all about – coping with variety and difference. Maybe our world would be a very boring place if we all believed the same thing, but maybe not of course. You should now have a good grasp of the basics of Christianity which you can follow up according to your own tastes, wherever that might take you. Hopefully you've been given a toolkit to help you work through the claims of the Christian faith and also put your own beliefs, or lack of them, to the test.

Learning outcomes

There are slight differences between Intermediate 1, 2 and Higher. Make sure your teacher has the latest arrangements documents from the SQA or check them yourself at *www.sqa.org.uk*. To help you, the differences in wording for the World Religions Unit have been put in bold below.

Intermediate 1

1 Demonstrate knowledge and understanding of religious beliefs.

2 Explain the way in which sacred writings, symbols and practices relate to religious beliefs.

3 Express reasoned opinions about the influence of religious beliefs on the lives of members of religious communities.

Intermediate 2

1 Demonstrate knowledge and understanding of religious beliefs.

2 **Explain religious beliefs by examining sources**.

3 **Justify conclusions** about the influence of religious beliefs on the lives of members of religious communities.

Higher

1 Demonstrate knowledge and understanding of religious beliefs.

2 **Analyse** religious beliefs by examining sources.

3 **Evaluate** the influence of religious beliefs on the lives of members of religious communities.

Depth, Breadth, Length

Sounds a bit like a swimming pool, but what are we really on about here?

The differentiating factor between Intermediate 1, 2 and Higher can probably be summed up in the three words: breadth, length and depth. The further away from Intermediate 1 you get the less descriptive you get and the more analytical you're meant to become. This means that you'll probably go into more *depth* in a topic the closer you get to Higher – analysing the whole thing just a little bit more fully and a little bit deeper. You'll also be expected to show more knowledge and understanding the closer you get to Higher. At Intermediate 1 you may take into account one Christian viewpoint, at Higher it's likely that you'll take a range of different viewpoints into account. This could be thought of as *breadth*. Finally, you should probably just know more at Higher than at Intermediate 1. You should be able to cover more areas of study and have a wider understanding of those areas – this could be thought of as *length*.

The split of marks in the Unit Assessments (NABs to you) reflects this idea as follows:

	Knowledge and Understanding	Analysis and Evaluation
Intermediate 1	70%	30%
Intermediate 2	60%	40%
Higher	60%	40%

As for the exam, sorry but there are no past papers and won't be for a while yet. Your teacher will have a Specimen Exam Paper from the SQA. This will help them to make up the prelim and give you an idea of what the actual exam might be like. This is probably on the SQA website too – check it out. This will show you what marks are available for KU and AE – remember to match your answer to the marks available!

Sample Assessment Questions (with sample answers)

Here are three sample assessment questions with three sample marking schemes. These are in note-form to give you an idea of the kind of thing which should be included in a good answer. Remember that how clearly you express yourself *does* matter. At Higher there is an example of a question which could equally well appear in a NAB as in the final examination!

Intermediate 1

Reminder: *You should choose this section if you have studied **Christianity** in the World Religions Unit. Answer **BOTH** questions (**1** and **2**) in this section of the paper.*

Question 1 – The Means

Instructions: *Look at the following stimulus then answer **all** parts of Question 1 (a)–(d). The number of marks available for each part is indicated. Use these as a guide to the amount of detail you should include in your answer.*

Stimulus

(a) Describe what the women found in the tomb when they went to anoint the body of the crucified Jesus
(2 marks)   KU

(b) What did the women do after they left the tomb?
(1 mark)   KU

(c) Describe **two** consequences of the Resurrection of Jesus for Christians
(4 marks)   KU

(d) 'The Resurrection of Jesus is the most important event in the story of Jesus'
Why might a Christian agree with this statement?
(3 marks)   AE

(Total 10 marks)

Question 2 – The Human Condition

Instructions: Read the **statement** below then answer the ***question*** that follows.

Statement:

"The Bible teaches that when man was first made (created) by God the relationship between man and God was perfect...... All we had to do was choose to stay in relationship with God"
Evangelical Christian view at www.sseconline.com/WhatWeBelieve.html

(a) Describe how God created Adam according to the Genesis story.
(3 marks)   KU

(b) What did God tell Adam not to do?
(1 mark)   KU

(c) Describe the events leading to Adam disobeying God.
(3 marks) KU

(d) For Christians, what was the significance of this disobedience?
(3 marks) AE

(Total 10 marks)

Sample Answers

Question 1

(a)

◆ Tomb was empty leaving only the linen cloths behind

◆ May mention young man dressed in white inside tomb

◆ May mention appearance of angel as in Matthew's gospel

(b)

◆ Departed with great joy

- Went to tell the disciples

- Or Mark's account where they left afraid saying nothing to anyone

- May mention conversation with angel and/or "gardener"

(c)

- Proves that Jesus was who he was claimed to be

- Fulfillment of his and OT prophecies

- Proves the power of Jesus

- Proof that death is not the end/Jesus has power over death etc

- Christians can share in the benefits of the resurrection

- Overturns Adam's disobedience by obeying God even to death

(d)

- Development of KU points in previous question eg

- This shows that Jesus was the Son of God/God incarnate and so proof of his divine nature

- It is the completion of God's attempts to re-establish the relationship between him and his creation

- It finally overturns the consequences of the fall

- It means that for Christians, death is not the end and the Resurrection shows that eternal life is possible by sharing in the acceptance of death by Jesus and so obeying God's will

Question 2

(a)

- Completes the creation of everything else

- Forms Adam from dust

- Breathes the breath of life into Adam

- Makes Adam in his own image

(b)

- Not to eat from the tree of knowledge of good and evil (because if you do that day you will die)

(c)

- Creation of Eve

- Temptation of Eve by serpent (you will not die if you eat of the tree/you will become like God with your eyes open)

◆ Eve eats the fruit

◆ Tempts Adam who also eats the fruit

(d)

◆ Practical consequences eg becoming aware of nakedness/feeling ashamed/hiding from God/banishment from Garden

◆ Punishment Eve – Childbirth pain/Adam – hard labour/Serpent eat dust crawl on belly

◆ Death enters as a result of the fall

◆ God and man separated by Adam's disobedience

◆ Effects of disobedience extended to all creation

◆ Original sin and its consequences

Intermediate 2

Reminder: *You should choose this section if you have studied **Christianity** in the World Religions Unit. Answer **ALL questions** in this section of the paper.*

Question 1 – The Goals

Instructions: *Read the following source and then answer **all** parts of Question 1 **(a)–(g)**. The number of marks available for each part is indicated. Use these as a guide to the amount of detail you should include in your answer.*

Source

> 'I was hungry and you fed me, thirsty and you gave me a drink; I was a stranger and you received me in your homes, naked and you clothed me; I was sick and you took care of me, in prison and you visited me.'
>
> "The righteous will then answer him, 'When, Lord, did we ever see you hungry and feed you, or thirsty and give you a drink? When did we ever see you a stranger and welcome you in our homes, or naked and clothe you? When did we ever see you sick or in prison, and visit you?'
>
> Matthew 25.35–39

(a) What answer was given to the question at the end of this source?
(1 mark) KU

(b) Describe the consequences of failing to help others given by this source
(3 marks) KU

(c) Describe two Christian understandings of hell.
(4 marks) KU

(d) How might belief in heaven and hell affect a Christian's lifestyle?
(4 marks)   AE

(e) In what different ways do Christians understand the idea of 'eternal life'?
(4 marks)   KU
(2 marks)   AE

(f) How might Christians show concern for others?
(4 marks)   KU

(g) 'To get into heaven you have to do good deeds'
Would all Christians agree with this statement?
Give reasons for your answer
(2 marks)   KU
(6 marks)   AE

(Total 32 marks)

Sample Answers

(a)

◆ I say to you, as you did it to the least of these, you did it to me (no need to quote directly just state the idea that Jesus was comparing the 'least' with himself)

(b)

◆ Depart from Jesus

◆ Sent to the eternal flames prepared for devil and his angels

◆ Eternal punishment for those who didn't help (and eternal life for those who did)

(c)

◆ Literal understanding – place of fire and punishment and eternal torture/torment

◆ Governed by the devil

◆ No chance of escape from it

◆ Symbolic understanding – place where God is absent and the lack of the presence of God is punishment in itself

(d)

◆ May choose to want to do good/avoid wrongdoing in the hope that this might help to 'get into' heaven and avoid hell (any example of such doing good)

◆ May think carefully about belief if view that 'good works' are not sufficient to achieve a place in heaven

◆ May describe idea of being 'born again' as a way of ensuring acceptance into the Kingdom of God

- Could answer that they won't affect lifestyle at all because Christians believe that God is completely forgiving and so hell is not possible

- May answer that lack of any real knowledge of the existence of either means that life should be lived according to the example of Jesus and not in anticipation of any reward or punishment

(e)

- Living eternally in the presence of God

- Description of the Kingdom of God – where justice, equality, peace etc are all present

- Life after death descriptions as in heaven hell

- May make some reference to Judgment/Judgment day

- Sharing in the benefits brought about by the Resurrection of Jesus and the overturning of Adam's disobedience with all the consequences which follow from that

- Description of the concepts of being 'born again'

- Can begin before death as a new spiritual relationship with God based on a re-establishment of the proper relationship between God and his creation

(f)

- Any examples of social action ranging from helping others at a Church club to involvement in world politics

- May simply be giving to charity or working in a community for the benefit of others

- Can also be simply living a considerate life in relation to helping other people as necessary

(g)

- *Agree* – Christians should life a life of concern for others as examples of the Kingdom of God here and now. Living the way God wants more likely to get you 'into' heaven than living a selfish life – any discussion of the concept of justification by works. Helping others creates God's Kingdom and shows that you have accepted the obedience of Jesus in overturning the consequences of the fall – so you will share in the benefits of this acceptance.

- *Disagree* – Works never enough to get 'into' heaven – ie you can never be 'good' enough to get into heaven. Must accept God (possible discussion of being born again) and believe in Jesus as Lord and Saviour etc – any discussion of the concept of justification by faith alone. Believing the right things shows that you have accepted Jesus and so you will share in his acceptance of God's will.

- For full marks it would be best for your answer to show the link between faith and good works – ie that believing the right things will automatically lead to good works and without these good works it is doubtful that you believe the right things!

Higher

Reminder: *You should choose this section if you have studied **Christianity** in the World Religions Unit. Answer **BOTH** questions (**1** and **2**) in this section of the paper.*

Question 1

Instructions: *Read the following source then answer **all** parts of Question 1 **(a)–(e)**. The number of marks available for each part is indicated. Use these as a guide to the amount of detail you should include in your answer.*

Hebrews 2: 14–18

Since the children, as he calls them, are people of flesh and blood, Jesus himself became like them and shared their human nature. He did this so that through his death he might destroy the Devil, who has the power over death, and in this way set free all those who were slaves all their lives because of their fear of death. For it is clear that it is not the angels that he helps. Instead, as the scripture says, 'He helps the descendants of Abraham.' This means that he had to become like his brothers in every way, in order to be their faithful and merciful High Priest in his service to God, so that the people's sins would be forgiven. And now he can help those who are tempted, because he himself was tempted and suffered.

(a) What do Christians mean by 'shared their human nature'?
    (4 marks)   KU

(b) 'Through his death he might destroy the Devil, who has power over death . . .'

    According to Christians, what can Jesus achieve through his death?
    (4 marks)   KU

(c) Explain how Christians see Jesus' death as a sacrifice.
    (6 marks)   (2KU, 4AE)

(d) Explain what Christians mean by salvation.
    (8 marks)   (4KU, 4AE)

(e) How can Christians overcome death?
    (3 marks)   KU

(Total 25 marks)

Question 2

Instructions: *Read the* **statement** *below then answer the* **question** *that follows.*

Statement:

To be considered a Christian you must accept Jesus as the new Adam.'

Explain how a Christian might respond to this statement.
(15 marks)   (5KU, 10AE)

(Total 15 marks)

Sample Answers

Question 1

(a)

◆ Jesus becomes human.

◆ This = Incarnation, God in human flesh.

◆ So God experiences human life first-hand.

◆ In becoming a human he can put right the human mistakes made at the Fall.

◆ As a human he can therefore mend the relationship between God and mankind.

◆ Could mention something about human nature being 'in the image of God' and all that this potentially means.

(b)

◆ Jesus achieves power over death.

◆ Death comes in through Adam's failure – is defeated through Jesus' success.

◆ Takes power away from the Devil who successfully tempted Adam into disobedience.

◆ So robs the Devil of his power.

◆ Death acts as a sacrifice to pay the price of sin.

◆ Shows that death is not the end and so frees people from fear of death and therefore its hold over mankind.

(c)

◆ Jesus is a sacrificial lamb – paying the price of sin.

◆ Jesus stands in and takes the punishment which humans should rightly get.

◆ Therefore returns God and mankind to original state of relationship – they are now at one – atonement theories.

- Mention of comparison with Old Testamant ideas of sacrifice and atonement.

- Washing away the stain of original sin through the shedding of his blood.

- God and mankind's separation is so significant that it needs such an extreme act to put it right.

- May show further evaluation of some issues – e.g. why God needed to pay himself and even so why it needed to be such a gruesome method of payment.

(d)

- Mankind fallen – needs to be redeemed.

- 'Being saved' is both from separation from God and also from the consequences of sin – i.e. death and suffering.

- Salvation leads to eternal life (explained) which can begin now.

- May make reference to, and analysis, of the Christian concept of being born again.

- Example, teaching and sacrifice of Jesus all part of the process of salvation.

- Importance of human free choice in deciding whether to accept Jesus as Saviour or not.

(e)

- By accepting Jesus as Saviour and so ...

- Sharing in the benefits of his yes to God.

- This results in the same benefits which Jesus experienced – i.e. power over death.

- Discussion of Resurrection of Jesus in relation to personal resurrection.

- Death not the end if eternal life can begin now.

Question 2

(KU) Knowledge and Understanding

- Explanation of the events of and meaning of The Fall.

- Therefore what the original Adam's choice was, why he did it and what it led to.

- Way in which Jesus can be considered the new Adam – a special creation – sent with a mission – given freedom to accept or reject God – comparisons of relationship between God/Adam and God/Jesus.

(AE) Analysis and Evaluation

- Jesus as new Adam overturns Adam's choice and therefore rejects sin and its consequences.

◆ Restores relationship between God and mankind.

◆ Christian life should aim to live in relationship with God – can do so if the meaning of the coming of Jesus is accepted, believed and lived.

◆ By accepting Jesus as Saviour, individual Christian states that s/he agrees with Jesus' choice and wishes to make the same choice – so has accepted God and restored his/her own relationship with God.

◆ Some discussion possible about what it means to be a Christian, including some possible variety across Christian denominations.

◆ Some discussion of the whole justification by faith/works issue possible.

◆ A good answer can be one-sided provided the line of argument is strong – though some evidence of taking an alternative view is often helpful – for example, stating that this is a doctrinal point and being a Christian doesn't depend on accepting doctrine, but on believing and living a good life as a consequence – so one can still be considered a Christian even if you have never given a great deal of thought to the deeper implications of what it might mean for Jesus to be the new Adam.

◆ At Higher level, backing up argument with relevant Christian sources is always advisable.

Final words

Your teacher will go over the exam technique until you're really quite sick of it so let's not do that here. Just remember that, specific to this course, you're really being expected to show the following things:

◆ That you have a knowledge and understanding of Christian beliefs.

◆ That you can back this up using relevant Christian sources either primary (The Bible; Church teachings/Tradition and the like) or secondary (comments and writings by Christians about their understanding of the faith).

◆ That you know and can discuss how all of this affects Christians as individuals and in groups in everyday life.

Remember that you have been learning about what Christians believe and do. You might be asked to express your own view on that in an assessment. You might not. Just make sure you know when to and when not to – and if you do, always do so in a reasonable way showing that you have benefited from a year's study of the topic!

Also, remember that when the exam is over you don't have to forget it all when you hand this book back to your teacher. Learning should go on throughout your whole life. Christianity, like all religions (and so RMPS) is about humanity's search for meaning, value and purpose in life. You're human. Keep searching.

INDEX

Index

Index